Little

Gulf Coast

Seafood Cookbook

Little Gulf Coast

Seafood Cookbook

By Kent Whitaker

Great American Publishers

www.GreatAmericanPublishers.com

TOLL-FREE 1.888.854.5954

Recipe Collection © 2017 by Great American Publishers

501 Avalon Way Suite B • Brandon, MS 39047
TOLL-FREE 1-888-854-5954 • www.GreatAmericanPublishers.com

ISBN 978-1-934817-33-9

by Kent Whitaker

Layout & Design by Nichole Stewart

First Edition

10 9 8 7 6 5 4 3 2 1

Every effort has been made to ensure the accuracy of the information provided in this book.
However, dates, times, and locations are subject to change.
Please call or visit websites for up-to-date information before traveling.

To purchase books in quantity for corporate use, incentives, or fundraising,
please call Great American Publishers at 888-854-5954.

Dedication

This book is dedicated to my wife Ally. The only other person I know who enjoys sand and sun as much I do. Ally and I, together, dedicate this tropical-sunscreen-scented culinary journal to our son Macee and our beach pups—Moses, Lucy, and King.

Macee and Friend Surfing

Introduction

I owe my love of the Gulf Coast to my parents; Eli and Arleta. Family visits were often filled with fun on the beach as Mom always loved planning for visits to coastal parks and museums. She was a school teacher with three sons so she searched for places such as the USS Alabama that would keep our attention. We all love the beach and I often wonder if Dad ever grew tired of us boys using his back as a surf board.

Sometimes, when the typical afternoon rains came, we played ski ball under tin roofed amusement centers. Evenings included visits to favorite restaurants followed by crab hunts with our flashlights. Those were the days. My brothers, Scot and Ty, and I were raised right.

My wife Allyson grew up as a beach kid, as well. My mother-in-law, "Momma Joan," says there was no doubt her daughter loved the water. "When she was a little girl, Allyson would leave a trail of clothes across the sand as she ran to the beach. The car was barely stopped before she was off running towards the water." It seems Allyson and her sisters and brother were also raised right.

Allyson and I have now built our own collection of coastal memories. Everything above still applies... except there are no longer any tin-roofed outdoor fun centers. We love having fun in the sun, digging our toes in the sand, cooling off in the gulf waters, and sitting on the beach at sunset. I'm a lover of history and especially military history. There is so much fascinating history to find on the Gulf Coast that I have included a few profiles throughout the book of interesting historical places to visit including the USS Alabama Battleship Memorial Park which is still one of my favorite destinations.

Of course Allyson and I also love seeking out the best seafood we can find along the Gulf Coast. Over the years, I have collected, tested and developed countless seafood dishes that we enjoy making at home. As I share my collection with you, I hope you enjoy these tasty dishes from, and inspired by, the Gulf Coast. Now, it's time to get cooking... and eating... See ya at the dinner table.

Buying Fresh Seafood

Here are some quick tips from the USDA that will help you select the best seafood possible.

- Only buy fish that is refrigerated or displayed on a thick bed of fresh ice that is not melting (preferably in a case or under some type of cover).
- Fish should smell fresh and mild, not fishy, sour, or ammonia-like.
- A fish's eyes should be clear and bulge a little.
- Whole fish and fillets should have firm, shiny flesh and bright red gills, free from milky slime.
- The flesh should spring back when pressed.
- Fish fillets should display no discoloration, darkening, or drying around the edges.
- Shrimp flesh should be translucent and shiny, with little or no odor.
- Some refrigerated seafood may have time/temperature indicators on their packaging, which show if the product has been stored at the proper temperature. Always check the indicators when they are present, and only buy seafood if the indicator shows the product is safe to eat.

Selecting Shellfish

Follow these general guidelines for safely selecting shellfish.

- Look for tags on sacks or containers of live shellfish (in the shell) and labels on containers or packages of shucked shellfish. These tags and labels contain specific information about the product, including the processor's certification number. This means the shellfish were harvested and processed in accordance with national shellfish safety controls.
- Throw away clams, oysters, and mussels if their shells are cracked or broken.
- Do a "Tap Test." Live clams, oysters, and mussels will close up when the shell is tapped. If they don't close when tapped, do not select them.
- Check for Leg Movement. Live crabs and lobsters should show some leg movement. They spoil rapidly after death, so only live crabs and lobsters should be selected and prepared.

USDA

Seafood Cooking Tips from the Pros

When putting my tips for cooking seafood into words, I decided to do what I tell my readers to do. ASK. So here are some tips from the Florida Bureau of Seafood and Aquaculture Marketing.

- Finfish should be cooked only until it flakes easily with a fork—the flesh will be firm and have an opaque, white look throughout.

- The 10 minute rule is a good starting guideline to use when baking, broiling, grilling, steaming, and poaching fish. Measure your fish at the thickest part and cook 10 minutes per inch of thickness at 400° to 450°. Add 5 additional minutes to total cooking time when fish is cooked in a sauce or in foil.

- Seafood will continue cooking after it has been removed from the heat, so remember to plan for this in your cooking time.

- Shellfish should be cooked until it becomes opaque throughout—it will not flake. Additional cooking will give you a tough product with a less desirable taste and texture.

- Shrimp and lobster turn red and the flesh becomes purely opaque. Shrimp cooks quickly (2 to 3 minutes).

- Scallops turn opaque and firm.

- Shucked oysters and clams are done when their edges curl.

- When working with clams, mussels, and oysters, their shells pop open when they're done (about 5 minutes). Discard those that stay closed.

Florida Bureau of Seafood and Aquaculture Marketing

Cape San Blas Shrimp Wings

Ally and I ate the hottest hot sauce ever with an order of shrimp during a visit to Cape San Blas. We enjoyed it so much, I made my own version. And, by the way, shrimp don't have wings.

1 stick butter
½ cup barbecue sauce
⅓ cup hot sauce
1 teaspoon garlic powder
¼ cup minced onion
1 pound medium or jumbo shrimp, peeled and deveined
1 tablespoon oil
1 tablespoon Cajun seasoning

Melt butter in a large saucepan; add barbecue sauce, hot sauce, garlic powder and onion. Bring to a boil then remove from heat. In a skillet, brown shrimp slightly in oil and Cajun seasoning; remove and toss shrimp into sauce mix. Serve with carrots, celery and a cold beverage.

Whole Gulf Shrimp Spring Rolls

20 large fresh Gulf shrimp
3 tablespoons hoisin sauce
2 tablespoons soy sauce
½ tablespoon brown sugar
2 to 3 teaspoons water
20 small wonton wrappers or spring roll wraps

Peel shrimp, leaving tail on; devein. Slice each shrimp partially through center to straighten. (Don't cut too deep so they don't break in half.) Place shrimp in a large bowl. Combine hoisin sauce, soy sauce, brown sugar and water in a small bowl. Pour over shrimp, gently tossing to coat evenly. Place a shrimp on a wrapper and fold corner, then gently straighten shrimp and roll wrapper to cover shrimp leaving tail exposed. Work in batches wrapping only the shrimp you can fry at a time to prevent wraps from getting soggy. Fry in hot oil 3 to 5 minutes or until wrapper is crunchy and golden. Serve hot with your favorite sauce.

Crab Jalapeño Poppers

If you don't like black olives, leave them out. It's all about a flavor combination that your taste buds will enjoy.

12 large (or 24 small) jalapeño peppers
½ pound cooked crabmeat
1 (8-ounce) package cream cheese, softened
⅓ cup shredded Cheddar cheese
3 tablespoons chopped black olives
⅓ cup minced onion
⅓ cup bacon bits
2 teaspoons paprika

Using protective gloves, slice jalapeños in half lengthwise and remove seeds. (If desired, parboil them a minute to blanch, but do not fully cook.) Mix crabmeat, creamed cheese, shredded cheese, olives, onion and bacon bits together; stuff jalapeño halves. Sprinkle with paprika. Bake at 325° (400° if you blanch the peppers) until cheese bubbles.

Bishop's Palace

The Bishop's Palace of Galveston is also known as "Gresham's Castle." The mansion is a 19,082 square-foot Victorian-style house built between 1887 and 1893. Walter Gresham, a lawyer and politician in Galveston, built the massive stone home for his wife and nine children. Gresham fought in the Civil War, earned a law degree, and served in the United States Congress. In 1900, a massive hurricane devastated the coastline and much of Galveston, causing 6,000 to 12,000 deaths. Gresham's Castle withstood the hurricane and the Gresham family opened their home to survivors. Gresham passed away in 1920, and the Roman Catholic Diocese of Galveston purchased the house in 1923, using it as a residence for Bishop Christopher E. Byrne. The diocese opened the mansion to the public in 1963 when its main offices moved to Houston. Today the mansion is owned by the Galveston Historical Foundation. Self-guided tours are available daily.

Bishop's Palace

1402 Broadway Avenue J • Galveston, Texas 77550

(409) 762-2475 • www.galvestonhistory.org

Coastal Crab Dip

There are a couple of ways to make crab dip. One is made in the oven and served hot. This version is served cold and is perfect for spring and summer meals served with crackers, veggies, or toasted bread. Fresh blue crabmeat from the Gulf of Mexico makes this recipe amazing!

8 ounces fresh blue crabmeat
1 (8-ounce) package cream cheese, softened
1½ tablespoons milk
2 teaspoons Worcestershire sauce
2 teaspoons Dijon mustard
1 teaspoon prepared horseradish
1½ tablespoons minced red bell pepper
1½ tablespoons minced green onion
1 teaspoon Cajun seasoning
2 teaspoons seafood seasoning
Salt and pepper to taste

Combine crabmeat, cream cheese, milk, Worcestershire sauce, Dijon mustard and horseradish in blender or food processor and blend until creamy. Spoon into a bowl and stir in remaining ingredients. Cover and chill in refrigerator 1 to 2 hours before serving. For a chunkier version, simply skip blender/food processor step and mix in a bowl.

Seafood Paté

You can call this recipe a paté or a seafood cheese ball. All I know is that it's perfect for spreading over crackers or lightly toasted, thin-sliced French bread.

1 pound cooked fish (or crabmeat)
3 tablespoons lemon juice
1 (8-ounce) package cream cheese, softened
1 tablespoon sour cream
½ stick butter, softened
1 tablespoon lemon pepper seasoning
½ tablespoon allspice
Salt and pepper to taste
1 tablespoon parsley flakes

Flake fish, removing bones and skin. Place everything, except parsley, in food processor; blend until a paste forms. For a chunky version, place everything in a bowl and mash with fork or spoon to desired texture. Stir in parsley flakes. Remove; place in a bowl and chill until firm.

Red Snapper Pimento Cheese with Bacon and Jalapeños

Pimento cheese is already enjoyed across the South as a spread, in sandwiches, and even for topping off a tasty burger. The addition of fresh red snapper, bacon and a pinch of jalapeño sets this recipe above the rest.

½ to ¾ cup (about 1 fillet) cooked and flaked red snapper, more if desired
1 cup shredded sharp Cheddar cheese
1 cup shredded Colby Jack cheese
1½ cups mayonnaise
2 to 3 tablespoons sour cream
⅓ cup real bacon bits
2 tablespoons minced jalapeño pepper
2 teaspoons hot sauce
1 teaspoon seafood seasoning
Cracked black pepper to taste
Garlic powder (optional)
1 (4-ounce) jar pimentos, well drained

Crumble red snapper; set aside. In a bowl, combine cheeses, mayonnaise, sour cream, bacon bits, jalapeños, hot sauce, seafood seasoning and black pepper; mix. Gently fold red snapper and pimentos into cheese mixture. Cover; chill before serving.

Easy Crawfish and Black Bean Nachos

Crawfish is a delicacy found along the Gulf Coast states and is often a staple for Cajun and Creole style cooking. This recipe is perfect for a fast appetizer.

1 pound cooked crawfish meat
1 bag tortilla chips
1 (15-ounce) can black beans, rinsed and drained
2 cups shredded Cheddar cheese
1 cup chunky salsa

Preheat oven to 350°. Chop crawfish, and set aside. Spread tortilla chips onto large, nonstick cookie sheet. Top with about a third of the cheese. Then top with half of the beans and salsa. Repeat layers then top with remaining cheese. Bake just until cheese is melted. Serve hot.

Ally's Key West Conch Fritter

This recipe is inspired by the great conch dishes Ally enjoyed in the Florida Keys. Conch meat is almost always imported, now, due to restrictions and low numbers. If you can't find conch meat, use crab, scallops or even fish. It all works well.

1 pound conch meat (or seafood)
⅔ cup all-purpose flour
2 eggs, beaten
½ cup milk
1 (4-ounce) can green chiles
Salt and pepper to taste
Cayenne pepper to taste
Dash sugar
Oil for frying

In a bowl, combine all ingredients; mix well. Add more milk, if needed, for a thick, chunky batter-like mix. Spoon into hot oil; fry until golden, turning as needed. Drain on paper towels. Serve hot.

Sweet Buttermilk Mullet Fritters

The first time I went fishing in the Gulf of Mexico, actually along the shore, my dad and grandfather used some small shiny fish as bait. They called them salt water "white fish." I eventually found out these small fish were mullet. But, if you've been around the gulf near Mississippi, you may have heard them called "Biloxi Bacon."

1 pound mullet fillets
½ cup self-rising cornmeal
½ cup self-rising flour
½ cup buttermilk
1 clove garlic, minced
½ cup minced sweet onion
¼ cup finely chopped carrot

1½ tablespoons chopped parsley
½ tablespoon sugar
2 teaspoons hot sauce
2 teaspoons seafood seasoning
1 large egg, beaten
Oil for frying

Chop mullet; set aside. In a large bowl, combine cornmeal, flour, buttermilk, garlic, onion, carrot, parsley, sugar, hot sauce, seafood seasoning and egg; mix well. Add mullet; mix well to further break it up. Heat oil in a heavy saucepan or deep fryer to 350°. Drop small amounts, about the size of a walnut, carefully into hot oil. Fry until golden brown turning and spinning to cook evenly (cooking time should be 3 to 4 minutes for a walnut-sized portion). Remove from oil; drain on rack over paper towels before serving.

GulfQuest: National Maritime Museum of the Gulf of Mexico

The National Maritime Museum of the Gulf of Mexico, also known as GulfQuest, is located in Mobile, Alabama. The museum combines state of the art technology with historical storytelling about Gulf Coast trade, shipwrecks, maritime commerce, shipbuilding, marine and coastal environments, and much more. The massive facility, which opened in 2015, has quickly become a tourist favorite. GulfQuest features 90 interactive exhibits, simulators, displays, and theaters. You can learn about everything from the earliest trade routes along the Gulf Coast to navigating a modern, computerized container ship. The museum is designed to involve the visitors of all ages and make you feel a part of things rather than viewing from behind traditional museum barriers. You may also enjoy ever-changing traveling exhibits, the ship's store, and The Galley featuring waterfront and outdoor dining.

GulfQuest: National Maritime Museum of the Gulf of Mexico

155 South Water Street • Mobile, Alabama 36602

(251) 436-8901 • www.gulfquest.org

Tapas-Style Creole Crab Balls with Dijon Rémoulade Sauce

1 pound crabmeat, cooked and flaked
1 cup panko breadcrumbs, divided
3 tablespoons mayonnaise
2½ tablespoons finely chopped red bell pepper
2 green onions, finely chopped
1 tablespoon finely chopped celery
½ tablespoon Creole seasoning
1 egg, beaten
1 teaspoon pepper
1 teaspoon seafood seasoning
2 teaspoons hot sauce

Preheat oven to 375°. Combine crab with about three quarters of the breadcrumbs (save some breadcrumbs in a shallow dish); add mayonnaise, red bell pepper, green onions, celery, Creole seasoning, egg, pepper, seafood seasoning and hot sauce. Mix, cover and chill 10 minutes to firm up slightly. Shape into walnut-sized portions; roll in remaining panko. Bake on nonstick baking sheet 20 to 25 minutes until golden brown and firm. Serve hot with Dijon Rémoulade Sauce.

Dijon Rémoulade Sauce:

⅔ cup mayonnaise
⅓ cup Dijon mustard
2 tablespoons sour cream
1 tablespoon finely chopped green onions
2 teaspoons parsley flakes
1 teaspoon tarragon
½ teaspoon chopped capers
½ teaspoon white wine vinegar

Combine all ingredients in a bowl; mix well. Cover; chill until ready to serve.

Crabmeat Balls

A cross between a meatball, hushpuppy and crab fritter. It all depends on how much breading and crab you use.

2 cups cooked and crumbled crabmeat
1 tablespoon Creole seasoning
3 tablespoons mayonnaise
1 tablespoon Worcestershire sauce
¼ cup chopped onion
2 eggs, beaten
1½ cups breadcrumbs
⅓ cup cornmeal
1 tablespoon parsley flakes
Oil for frying

Mix all ingredients; shape into small balls, about 1½-inches in diameter. Deep-fry 5 to 8 minutes until golden brown. Serve hot. You can also bake crab balls at 350° for 30 minutes or until golden brown.

Mississippi Mashed Seafood Tater Tots

3 cups leftover mashed potatoes
⅔ cup flaked crabmeat
½ cup cornmeal
¼ cup finely diced onion
1 teaspoon garlic powder
1 egg, beaten
½ cup breadcrumbs
Oil for frying
Cajun seasoning

In a bowl, combine potatoes, crabmeat, cornmeal, onion and garlic powder; form 1½-inch balls. Dip in egg, roll in breadcrumbs and fry in deep fryer so entire ball cooks evenly until golden brown. As soon as you remove balls from oil, sprinkle with Cajun seasoning. Drain; serve hot.

Slightly Spicy Panko Crab Cakes

1 pound flaked crabmeat, rinsed and checked for cartilage
3 tablespoons mayonnaise
4 eggs, beaten
1 tablespoon Worcestershire sauce
1 tablespoon hot sauce
½ tablespoon Dijon mustard
Butter for sautéing
⅓ cup finely chopped sweet onion
⅓ cup finely chopped green onion
⅓cup finely chopped red bell pepper
2 to 3 tablespoons finely chopped parsley
¼ tablespoon seafood seasoning, additional for sprinkling
Garlic powder to taste
Salt and pepper to taste
3 cups plain breadcrumbs, additional for dredging
Vegetable oil for frying

Combine crabmeat, mayonnaise, eggs, Worcestershire sauce, hot sauce and Dijon mustard in a large bowl; set aside. In a skillet, sauté onions and bell pepper in butter; stir in remaining seasonings and breadcrumbs. Form mixture into cakes of equal size. Dredge cakes in reserved breadcrumbs, place on cookie sheet with wax paper and chill 30 to 60 minutes in refrigerator. Cook in hot oil until golden brown, turn and cook until other side is golden. You can keep cooked crab cakes warm in oven on a cookie sheet while finishing remaining cakes.

Texas Coast Tortilla Chip Crab Cakes

3 slices bread, crust trimmed (white or wheat)
2 tablespoons milk
1 pound crabmeat
1 (4-ounce) can chopped green chiles
2 tablespoons mayonnaise
1 tablespoon Dijon mustard
½ tablespoon hot sauce
2 teaspoons seafood seasoning
½ tablespoon parsley flakes
½ tablespoon crushed red pepper
Tortilla chips, crushed
Oil for frying
Salsa for topping, warmed (optional)

Break bread into small pieces; moisten with milk. Combine with remaining ingredients, except crushed tortilla chips. Shape into patties; if too wet, mix in a few breadcrumbs. Press patties into crushed chips, covering evenly. Fry patties quickly in hot oil until brown. Top with a spoonful of warmed salsa, if desired.

Grilled Gator Bites with Tangy Orange Dipping Sauce

Gator meat is best when cooked as fresh as possible, but frozen gator meat can be saved for up to six months. Use with a marinade and don't overcook as it can become tough.

2 pounds alligator meat
½ cup orange juice
¼ cup steak marinade
¼ cup Italian seasoning
2 tablespoons light soy sauce
2 tablespoons brown sugar
1 teaspoon cumin
1 teaspoon Cajun seasoning

Cube alligator meat into 1-inch cubes; spread evenly in glass baking dish. In bowl, combine orange juice, steak marinade, Italian dressing, soy sauce, brown sugar, cumin and Cajun seasoning; mix well. Spread evenly over gator meat; turn to coat evenly. Cover; chill in refrigerator at least 1 hour. Grill, using a grilling basket or tray, over medium-high heat 4 to 5 minutes; turn and grill an additional 4 to 5 minutes. Serve gator bites hot with the Tangy Orange Dipping Sauce. Serve with carrot sticks or celery sticks similar to how you would Buffalo chicken wings.

Tangy Orange Dipping Sauce:

⅔ cup orange marmalade
⅓ cup taco sauce
1 tablespoon rice vinegar
1 tablespoon Dijon mustard
2 to 3 teaspoons red pepper flakes

Combine marmalade, taco sauce, rice vinegar, Dijon mustard and red pepper flakes in a bowl; mix well. Chill before serving.

Southern Fried Alligator

Once you've tried a basket of southern fried alligator nuggets, you'll push the chicken nuggets to the side . Of course gators don't have nuggets.

1½ pounds alligator
1 cup all-purpose flour plus more for dusting
1 cup cornmeal
1 (16-ounce) can ice cold beer
2 tablespoons honey
1 teaspoon cayenne pepper
2 tablespoons sugar

Preheat deep-fryer to 375°. Cube meat into 1- to 2-inch pieces, similar to chicken nuggets. Sizes can vary slightly. In a bowl, combine flour, cornmeal, beer, honey, cayenne and sugar; mix well. Lightly dust meat in flour; dip in batter allowing excess to drain off slightly. Carefully cook meat in small batches, turning as needed, for 6 to 8 minutes or until batter is golden brown. Drain on paper towels. Serve alligator nuggets on wax or brown paper in a bowl or basket with Easy Barbecue Ranch Sauce drizzled on top or in a bowl on the side.

Easy Barbecue Ranch Sauce

¾ cup ranch dressing
1¼ cups barbecue sauce

Combine ranch dressing and barbecue sauce in a bowl; mix. Chill before serving.

Crawdaddy's Gumbo

Crawdaddy's was one of my family's favorite restaurants. After it closed, Sam, the nice lady who owned it, was kind enough to give me her gumbo recipe. Thank you, Sam and Wes, for so many wonderful meals.

1½ pounds chicken pieces
3 quarts water
Salt and pepper to taste
½ cup oil
½ cup all-purpose flour
2 onions, finely chopped
2 ribs celery, chopped
1 large bell pepper, chopped
2 garlic cloves, minced

1 bay leaf
1 teaspoon cayenne pepper
1 teaspoon black pepper
2 teaspoons salt
Dash Worcestershire sauce
1½ pounds fresh okra, sliced
1 (16-ounce) can diced tomatoes
½ pound andouille sausage, sliced
½ to 1 pound crawfish tail meat

In a large stockpot, cook chicken in seasoned water over medium heat until done. Strain stock and set aside. Remove meat from bones and set aside. In a heavy Dutch oven, combine oil and flour. Cook over medium heat, stirring frequently until browned to make a dark brown roux. Add onions, celery, bell pepper and garlic; sauté until vegetables are tender, about 15 minutes. Add bay leaf and other spices, okra, tomatoes and chicken broth; bring to a slow boil. Cover and simmer 1½ to 2 hours, stirring occasionally. Add reserved chicken and sliced sausage; simmer 15 more minutes. Add crawfish and cook 8 to 10 minutes or just until crawfish are cooked through.

Coastal Crab Gumbo

Gumbo without a roux? Yes, Indeed. Give it a chance; it's delicious. There are more versions of gumbo than there are styles of swimsuits on any given Gulf Coast beach day. This is an easy gumbo recipe that works great with crab, shrimp, or even crawfish.

½ cup chopped onion
4 tablespoons butter or margarine
1 (15-ounce) can diced tomatoes
1 (6-ounce) can tomato paste
1 cup water
2 chicken bouillon cubes
2 teaspoons sugar
2 teaspoons salt
2 teaspoons black pepper
1 teaspoon garlic powder
1 cup sliced okra
¼ pound crab (or other seafood)
2½ cups prepared white rice

In a medium saucepan, brown onion in butter to golden brown. Add remaining ingredients, except rice. Cover and simmer 30 to 45 minutes. Add rice to gumbo just before serving, or serve gumbo over rice.

Easy Coastal Seafood Chowder

A good bowl of chowder is a great thing. This simple chowder makes a wonderful meal or appetizer using just about any seafood you prefer.

1 pound seafood (fish, shrimp or crab)
5 cups water
1 large baking potato, peeled and cubed
1 onion, finely diced
1 celery stalk, finely diced
½ stick butter
⅓ cup real bacon bits
1 teaspoon garlic
½ teaspoon lemon juice
Large dash Worcestershire sauce
1 cup milk
Salt and pepper to taste
Parsley

Clean and rinse seafood. Place in a large skillet with water; boil until seafood is done. If using fish, remove from water, flake fish, removing bones. Return back to water; add potato, onion, celery and butter. Cook until potatoes are tender. Add remaining ingredients, except parsley; allow chowder to thicken slightly before serving. Serve hot with parsley sprinkled on top.

Spicy Crab Soup

This great crab soup is full of flavor with a bit of bite.

2 cups crabmeat
1 (15-ounce) can whole-kernel corn, drained
½ tablespoon minced garlic
1 small onion, minced
2 tablespoons oil
½ cup minced celery
2 (14-ounce) cans chicken broth
1 (13.5-ounce) can coconut milk
1 cup water
⅓ cup hot sauce
1 tablespoon Cajun seasoning
½ tablespoon ginger
½ tablespoon chili powder
½ tablespoon brown sugar
Juice of ½ lemon or lime

Place crab and corn in a large pot and set aside. In a small skillet, brown garlic and onion in oil. Add celery, mix well and immediately add to pot with crab. Add remaining ingredients and simmer over medium-high heat 10 to 15 minutes. If desired, slowly stir in a spoonful of flour to thicken.

Gulf Coast Chopped Shrimp Bisque

Plan ahead if you make your own shrimp stock for this recipe. Much of the flavor for this bisque comes from the use of the shrimp heads, shells and tails.

Shrimp Stock:

1½ pounds raw medium Gulf Coast shrimp
1 stick butter
8 cups water
½ sweet onion
1 stalk celery, large chopped
½ tablespoon salt
½ tablespoon seafood seasoning
1 bay leaf
¼ tablespoon black pepper

Cut heads and tails off shrimp; remove legs and shells. Rinse shrimp; cover and chill while your stock is being made. Place shrimp heads, tails, shells and legs in a stockpot; add butter, water, onion, celery, salt, seafood seasoning, bay leaf and black pepper. You can also toss in the leaves from the celery stalk. Boil on high for 10 minutes; reduce heat to a simmer. When the simmer starts, skim the top of the stock for white fatty pieces. Cover; simmer 90 minutes. Remove from heat; carefully strain using a fine mesh strainer.

Bisque:

Oil or butter for sautéing
Reserved shrimp, lightly chopped
¼ cup minced onion
¼ cup minced bell pepper
Shrimp Stock
2 to 3 tablespoons all-purpose flour for bisque
1 cup cream
2 tablespoons tomato paste, substituting ketchup will add a bit of a sweeter taste
3 teaspoons paprika
2 teaspoons cayenne pepper
Extra paprika for garnish
Chopped shallots for garnish

In a skillet, sauté shrimp, onion and pepper in hot oil or butter. When shrimp edges are lightly browned, remove all from heat; set aside. In a stockpot, combine stock, flour, cream, tomato paste, paprika and cayenne pepper; simmer 30 minutes to thicken slightly. Stir in sautéed mixture; continue to cook over low for 5 minutes. Serve hot, garnished with a dash of paprika, chopped shallots or parsley leaves and a side of toasted crunchy French bread. For a smoother bisque, you can purée slightly in a blender or food processor.

Broiled Scallop and Portabella Mushroom Salad

This recipe, from the Florida Bureau of Seafood and Aquaculture Marketing, calls for Florida calico scallops. You can also use bay scallops as a substitution, if needed.

2 pounds Florida calico scallops
1 pound Florida Portabella mushrooms, sliced
1½ teaspoons ground allspice
1 teaspoon ground coriander
1 teaspoon marjoram
1 teaspoon salt
3 cups shredded arugula
1 head Florida romaine lettuce, torn

Preheat oven to broil. Arrange scallops and mushrooms on broiler pan; coat tops with allspice, coriander, marjoram and salt. Broil 3 to 4 inches from heat, for 5 to 6 minutes, or until scallops are opaque; drain. Transfer to a cool platter; chill 30 minutes. Arrange arugula and romaine on 6 chilled salad plates; top with scallops and mushrooms. Makes 6 servings.

Florida Bureau of Seafood and Aquaculture Marketing

Marinated Swordfish Salad

I asked a buddy what was his favorite fish. "Swordfish! When you get one on the line you better hold on!" This simple recipe, courtesy of the Florida Bureau of Seafood and Aquaculture Marketing, is packed with tons of flavor.

2 pounds Florida swordfish fillets
¼ cup olive oil
3 tablespoons wine vinegar
2 tablespoons capers
3 garlic cloves, minced
¼ cup chopped Florida green onions
2 teaspoons chopped cilantro
½ teaspoon dried basil
½ teaspoon salt
½ teaspoon white pepper
Your favorite salad greens

Cut swordfish into 1-inch pieces; broil, 3 to 4 inches from heat, 3 to 5 minutes or until flakes easily. Remove from heat, transfer to a cool plate and set aside. Combine remaining ingredients, except salad greens, in shallow container with a lid; mix well. Place fish in a single layer in marinade; close lid tightly. Chill 2 hours. Remove fish from marinade; arrange on salad greens. Makes 4 servings.

Florida Bureau of Seafood and Aquaculture Marketing

Biloxi Bacon Po-Boy with Fried Pickles and Jalapeños

"Biloxi Bacon" refers to mullet fish from the Gulf of Mexico. During the Great Depression, the fish were caught, cut into fillets, and slow smoked because the abundant number of mullet in the gulf made for a nice supply of affordable food. This Biloxi Bacon Po-Boy uses real bacon, and the fillet is fried not smoked. Fried pickles and jalapeños add a delicious crunch.

8 slices bacon
4 skinless mullet fillets, cut lengthwise for 8 pieces
2 eggs, lightly beaten
2 tablespoons milk
1 cup panko breadcrumbs
½ cup cornmeal
1 tablespoon seafood seasoning
Oil for frying
8 dill pickles, sliced lengthwise for 16 pieces
1 cup jalapeño slices
Flour for dusting
4 French bread deli-style hoagie buns, toasted
Lettuce
Sliced tomatoes
Creamy Coleslaw (page 139)
Dijon Rémoulade Sauce (page 23)

Cook bacon in a skillet; remove to drain on a paper towel, reserving 2 tablespoons drippings. Make a dredge by combining eggs, milk and reserved bacon drippings in a shallow dish or bowl. In a separate shallow dish, combine breadcrumbs, cornmeal and seafood seasoning. Heat oil to 350°. While oil heats, lightly dust fillets, pickles and jalapeño slices with flour, tapping off any excess. Dredge each dusted fillet in egg wash then cornmeal mixture. Cook in hot oil 4 to 5 minutes on each side or until crust is golden brown. Repeat process with pickles then jalapeños. Serve hot fillets on buns topped with bacon, lettuce, tomato, fried pickles and fried jalapeños. Top with Creamy Coleslaw and Dijon Rémoulade Sauce.

Blackened Catfish Hoagie with Creole Mustard Sauce

4 (6-ounce) skinless catfish fillets
1 tablespoon paprika
2 teaspoons each: dried thyme, onion powder and garlic powder
1 teaspoon each: salt, pepper and cayenne pepper
½ teaspoon sugar
4 hoagie rolls
Butter
Lettuce, sliced onion and sliced tomato

Preheat oven to 350°. Rinse fillets, pat dry using paper towels and place on a nonstick baking dish. In a bowl, combine paprika, thyme, onion powder, garlic powder, salt, pepper, cayenne and sugar to make blackening rub; evenly rub into each fillet. Bake 15 minutes or until fish flakes easily. Butter hoagie rolls; place in oven before removing catfish fillets. Serve fillets hot on buttered and toasted hoagie rolls with lettuce, onion and tomato and topped with Creole Mustard Sauce.

Creole Mustard Sauce:

⅔ cup mayonnaise
3 tablespoons Creole or spicy mustard
1 tablespoon sour cream (or ½ tablespoon milk)
1 teaspoon lemon juice

In a bowl, combine all ingredients. Chill before serving.

Seafood Po-Boy

Easy Po-Boy Sauce:

4 tablespoons mayonnaise
1½ tablespoons ketchup
2 tablespoons sweet pickle relish
1 tablespoon hot sauce
½ tablespoon lemon juice

Combine all and refrigerate while preparing Seafood Po-Boy.

Seafood Po-Boy:

1 cup crabmeat, shrimp, fish or your favorite seafood
Peanut oil for frying
2 cups all-purpose flour
1 teaspoon each: salt, black pepper and cayenne pepper
1 egg, beaten
¼ cup milk
French bread
Lettuce

Clean seafood and set aside to dry. Heat oil in a deep-fat fryer or deep skillet. Mix flour, salt and peppers in a shallow bowl. In another bowl, combine egg and milk. Dip seafood in egg mixture then roll lightly in flour mixture. Drop in hot oil and fry until golden brown. Remove to drain on paper towels. Coat French bread with Easy Po-Boy Sauce; top with lettuce and seafood. Serve hot.

1940 Air Terminal Museum

The 1940 Air Terminal Museum, located at William P. Hobby Airport, is where history comes alive in Houston, Texas. The restored Art Deco building served as a terminal for Houston air flight starting in the 1940's. A proposal to demolish the building in 1978 was beaten by local history organizations. The building sat vacant until work began, in 1998, to open the museum. The first phase of the museum officially opened in 2004. Today the 1940 Air Terminal Museum is a fun museum offering many exhibits focusing mainly on Houston's civil, commercial and recreational aviation history. You'll love the Starliner Theater with video presentations about the history of flight. A hanger houses several period aircraft as well as airport support vehicles. The monthly Fly-in, called "Wing and Wheels," has grown into a mini aviation show that people of all ages enjoy. Every month pilots fly their planes, often vintage or historic, to the tarmac to put them on display for visitors. The varied events at the museum also often include helicopters, military vehicles, show cars, show trucks, and traveling aviation exhibits.

1940 Air Terminal Museum

8325 Travelair Street • Houston, Texas 77061
(713) 454-1940 • www.1940airterminal.org

Pineapple Rum Grouper Cheddar Melts with Spicy Apricot Dipping Sauce

Sourdough bread gives this recipe a perfect hardy texture and taste.

4 skinless, boneless grouper fillets
Olive oil
2 teaspoons seafood seasoning
¼ cup pineapple-flavored rum

2 tablespoons lemon
8 Cheddar cheese slices
8 slices sourdough bread
Butter

In a glass baking dish, brush fillets with olive oil, season with seafood seasoning, and drizzle with pineapple-flavored rum and lemon juice. Marinate at least 30 minutes. Bake in 350° for 12 minutes or until fish flakes. Place hot fillets between 2 pieces of buttered sourdough bread wedged between 2 slices of Cheddar cheese. Brown each sandwich in a skillet until bread is golden and cheese is melted. Serve sandwiches hot with a side of Apricot Dipping Sauce.

Apricot Dipping Sauce:

1 cup apricot jam
½ stick butter
½ tablespoon hot sauce

In a saucepan, combine jam, butter and hot sauce. Simmer over low heat until jam melts and ingredients combine.

Open-Faced Halibut Sandwiches with Peach and Mango Salsa

Peach and Mango Salsa:

5 peaches, chopped
1 mango, peeled and chopped
1 large tomato, chopped
½ cup diced red onion
1 red bell pepper, diced

2 jalapeños, finely chopped
1½ tablespoons lemon juice
1 tablespoon honey
2 teaspoons dried cilantro

Combine salsa ingredients in a bowl; mix well. Cover and chill 30 minutes or longer. Stir again just before serving.

Halibut:

4 skinless halibut fillets
1 tablespoon lemon juice
1 tablespoon olive oil
3 teaspoons seafood seasoning
2 teaspoons paprika

2 teaspoons onion powder
2 garlic cloves, minced
1 teaspoon salt
1 teaspoon black pepper

Place fillets in a glass baking dish. Whisk remaining Halibut ingredients in a bowl. Pour half the marinade over fillets; flip and cover with remaining marinade. Cover dish and refrigerate while grill is heating. Brush grill grates with oil before grilling or use an oiled or nonstick grilling basket. Grill fillets over medium-high heat 3 to 4 minutes per side or until fish flakes easily.

French Bread:

4 French bread slices
Butter for grilling
Dash garlic powder
1 cup fresh spinach, stems removed and lightly shredded

Butter bread on one side; sprinkle very lightly with garlic powder. Grill, butter-side down, just long enough to get nice grill marks. Place spinach on French Bread; top with a halibut fillet fresh off the grill. Finish with Peach and Mango Salsa.

Blue Crab Salad Sandwich

Water chestnuts add an interesting flavor and the perfect amount of crunch to this delicious Blue Crab Salad.

1 pound fresh lump blue crabmeat, checked for shells
1 (8-ounce) can water chestnuts
½ cup mayonnaise
½ cup fine shredded carrots
2 teaspoons minced fresh chives
2 teaspoons freshly squeezed lemon juice
1 teaspoon seafood seasoning
1 teaspoon hot sauce
Texas toast, buttered and toasted
Parsley flakes for garnish

Place crabmeat in a bowl. Slightly chop water chestnuts into small pieces about the size of pencil eraser. Combine with remaining ingredients; stir to mix. Cover; chill before serving. Serve on buttered, toasted slices of Texas toast. Garnish with parsley flakes.

Easy Gulf Coast Shrimp Sliders

2 pounds medium shrimp, peeled, tailless and deveined
1 cup barbecue sauce
1 cup Oriental sweet chili sauce
2 cups shredded cabbage slaw mix
¼ to ½ cup mayonnaise
2 teaspoons sugar
1 teaspoon black pepper
2 packs sweet Hawaiian-style dinner rolls

Rinse, drain and place shrimp in a large bowl. In another bowl, combine barbecue sauce and sweet chili sauce. Pour the majority of sauce over shrimp; toss to coat evenly. Save remaining sauce mix for your baste. Combine cabbage, mayonnaise, sugar and black pepper in a bowl. Stir in ¼ cup mayonnaise and add more if desired. Cover and chill while you grill the shrimp.

Grill shrimp over medium-high heat using a grilling sheet, turning and basting as needed, for 8 minutes until shrimp is golden on the edges, opaque and cooked through. Discard any remaining sauce. Serve shrimp on sweet Hawaiian rolls topped with slaw.

Minced Gulf Shrimp Burgers

1½ pounds medium shrimp, peeled and deveined
2 teaspoons minced garlic
2 teaspoons lemon juice
2 slices wheat bread, torn into small pieces
⅓ cup mayonnaise
2 green onions, thinly sliced
3 tablespoons finely chopped red bell pepper
2 teaspoons seafood seasoning
Salt and pepper to taste
Butter or oil for frying
Buns, toasted
Lettuce
Sliced tomato
Tartar Sauce

Place shrimp, garlic and lemon juice in food processor; pulse 4 to 5 times. Add bread, pulsing several more times until well mixed. Spoon mixture into a bowl. Add mayonnaise, onion, bell pepper, seafood seasoning, salt and pepper; mix well. Spoon 4 to 6 equal portions onto foil or a cookie sheet coated with nonstick spray. Use a wet spoon to form portions into 1-inch-thick burgers. Cover with cling wrap; chill 30 minutes to an hour. In a nonstick skillet, heat butter or oil. Add burgers; cook over medium-high heat 4 to 5 minutes per side, turning once. Serve on toasted, buttered buns topped with lettuce, a tomato slice and tartar sauce.

Texas Coast Shrimp Scampi

This may very well be the easiest shrimp scampi recipe in the world... with a touch of Tex-Mex flavor.

1 tablespoon minced garlic
2 to 3 tablespoons butter
2 tablespoons olive oil
Coarse salt
¼ to ½ teaspoon red pepper flakes
1 pound medium shrimp, shelled and deveined
½ tablespoon chili powder
1 to 2 teaspoons cumin powder
½ cup white wine
Freshly ground black pepper to taste
2 tablespoons finely chopped parsley
1 tablespoon lemon juice
Chili powder for garnish

In a skillet, sauté garlic in butter and olive oil; season with salt to taste and red pepper. Add shrimp, chili powder, cumin and wine. Stir shrimp as they cook, coating evenly with butter and wine sauce. Cook about 5 minutes until wine cooks off and shrimp are opaque. Add pepper, parsley and lemon juice; stir to evenly coat shrimp. Remove from heat. Sprinkle with a small amount of chili powder just before serving. Delicious served with buttered and toasted Texas toast. Enjoy.

Time-Saver Pesto Shrimp and Pasta

This is a super easy recipe using ingredients you probably already have in your kitchen pantry. All you need is some fresh shrimp to get going.

1½ pounds small to medium shrimp, tailless, shelled and deveined
1 (10-ounce) package thin spaghetti noodles or angel hair pasta
2 tablespoons olive oil
1 cup chopped onion
½ cup thinly sliced red bell pepper
1 (10-ounce) package frozen peas
2 tablespoons pesto sauce
½ teaspoon minced garlic
Salt and pepper to taste
2 tablespoons chopped parsley
1 tablespoon Italian seasoning
Parmesan cheese for garnish

Rinse shrimp and set aside in a bowl. Cook pasta in salted water per package directions. Drain, reserving ½ cup cooking water. Heat olive oil In a large skillet; sauté onion until just tender. Stir in bell pepper, peas, pesto, garlic, salt and pepper. Cook until heated through, stirring as needed. Add shrimp; stir. Add parsley, Italian seasoning and reserved pasta water; stir well. Stir in pasta and cook just long enough to reheat. Serve hot sprinkled lightly with Parmesan cheese.

Key West Scallop and Chicken Pasta

Ally is a scallop nut; I created this recipe for her. We enjoy this made with a fruity white wine; the red wine is great for when the weather turns a little cooler.

2 cups scallops
2 cups cooked cubed chicken
1 tablespoon minced garlic
Olive oil
Italian seasoning to taste
1 (10-ounce) can diced tomatoes with chiles
½ cup white or red wine
1 (4.25-ounce) can sliced black olives, drained
1 (4-ounce) can sliced mushrooms, drained
1 (8-to 10-ounce) package Angel hair pasta, prepared

In a skillet over medium-high heat, sauté scallops, chicken and garlic in olive oil; season with Italian seasoning. When chicken is light golden brown, add tomatoes and wine. Reduce heat and simmer to reduce half the liquid. Add olives and mushrooms; cook 3 more minutes. Remove from heat and serve hot over angel hair pasta.

Bayou Big Easy Crawfish Alfredo

1 (12-ounce) package fettuccine, cooked and drained
1 teaspoon olive oil
½ tablespoon minced garlic
1 tablespoon minced onion
1 pound crawfish tail meat
1 (16-ounce) jar Alfredo sauce
1 (8-ounce) can green English peas, drained
1 tablespoon chopped parsley

Cook pasta according to directions; drain and return to pot. In a nonstick skillet, heat olive oil over medium heat; add garlic, onion and crawfish, searing 1 to 2 minutes until golden brown. Set aside. Add Alfredo sauce and peas to pasta. Cook over medium-high heat until warmed. Before serving, stir in crawfish and parsley. Serve hot.

Mexico Beach Butter Scallops

The Mexico Beach and Port St. Joe area of Florida are well known for their bay scallops.

1 pound scallops
1 teaspoon minced garlic
⅓ cup butter, melted
Lemon pepper seasoning to taste
1½ teaspoons chopped parsley

In a skillet over high heat, sauté scallops and garlic in butter. Cook scallops 3 minutes per side or until golden brown. Sprinkle with lemon pepper during last minute; add parsley. Serve hot over angel hair pasta.

Historic Pensacola

Historic Pensacola is an amazing combination of history and family-friendly tourism. The site, 8.5 acres, boasts 20-plus historic properties with 11 being open to the public. Located minutes from the Gulf Coast, Historic Pensacola includes four museums: the T.T. Wentworth, Jr. Florida State Museum, the Museum of Commerce, the Museum of Industry, and the Pensacola Children's Museum. All of the properties offer museum-like qualities with displays, interactive exhibits, living history events, and more. One popular stop for visitors is The Old Christ Church, which was built in 1832. It was once occupied by Union Troops during the Civil War. Now, like many of the other structures, it plays host to special events and weddings. Today, Historic Pensacola is run by the University of West Florida Historic Trust. The concept was made possible during the 1960's. Local residents, led by Mary Turner Rule, sought to preserve historic structures in and around Pensacola, including Seville Square and the Dorr House.

Historic Pensacola

120 Church Street • Pensacola, Florida 32502
(850) 595-5985 • www.historicpensacola.org

Kent's Shrimp, Chicken and Sausage Jambalaya

2 cups diced cooked chicken
½ cup oil
Salt and pepper to taste
2 cups sliced smoked sausage
1½ cups diced onions
½ cup diced red onion
1 red bell pepper, diced
1 green bell pepper, diced
1 cup chopped celery
½ cup diced tomato
1 stick butter
3 quarts water
1 beef bouillon cube
2 cups uncooked white rice
1 tablespoon minced garlic
¼ cup hot sauce
¼ cup Cajun seasoning
2 cups peeled deveined shrimp

In a large pot, brown chicken in oil with salt and pepper; add sausage, onions, peppers, celery and tomato. Cook until vegetables are soft. Add butter, water and remaining ingredients, except shrimp. Cook uncovered until rice is done. Add more hot sauce as desired. Add shrimp; cook 10 minutes before serving.

Gulf Coast Shrimp Jambalaya

1 cup chopped sweet onion
½ cup chopped celery
½ cup chopped green bell pepper
½ stick butter
3 cups chicken broth
1½ cups uncooked rice
½ tablespoon Creole seasoning
½ tablespoon hot sauce
2 teaspoons Worcestershire sauce
2 teaspoons cayenne pepper
2 (10-ounce) cans diced tomatoes with green chiles, drained
1½ pounds medium Gulf Coast shrimp, cooked, peeled and deveined
1½ cups frozen peas (or peas and carrots)

In a large nonstick pot or Dutch oven, sauté onion, celery and pepper in butter until tender. Carefully add chicken broth, rice, Creole seasoning, hot sauce, Worcestershire and cayenne pepper. Bring to a boil, cooking 5 minutes; reduce heat to low. Cover; cook 15 to 20 minutes or until rice is tender. (If you use brown or wild rice, cooking time will be longer and additional liquid may be needed.) Stir in tomatoes, shrimp and peas; cook until heated through. Serve hot.

Beach Grouper Packs

This recipe tastes best cooked on the beach over an open fire, but first make sure local laws allow beach cooking!

4 grouper fillets
½ lemon, juiced
1½ lemons, sliced into 8 thin slices
4 tablespoons chopped onion
4 tablespoons butter, melted
½ teaspoon garlic salt
½ teaspoon salt
½ teaspoon chili powder
1 teaspoon hot sauce
¼ teaspoon ground dry mustard
1 tablespoon chopped parsley

Place grouper fillets on individual squares of heavy-duty aluminum foil coated with nonstick spray. Top each with lemon juice and 2 slices lemon. Sprinkle evenly with chopped onion. Combine melted butter with remaining ingredients; drizzle evenly over fillets. Fold foil over fish and seal securely. Cook over open fire or on grill about 10 to 15 minutes, turning at least once for thicker fillets (thinner cuts may not need to be turned). Open foil to check for doneness. When fish flakes with a fork, it's ready. Serve hot.

Biloxi Mississippi Lighthouse

Biloxi Lighthouse, the only lighthouse located in the center of a busy highway, was erected in 1848 at a cost of $6,347 and was one of the first cast-iron lighthouses in the South. It also has the distinction of having more female light keepers than any other lighthouse in the country, including Mary Reynolds who lived in the keeper's house with a large family of orphaned children. After her husband died one year into service, Maria Younghans was the keeper for 53 years before her daughter, Miranda, took over after Maria retired at 72 years of age. Owned and Operated by the City of Biloxi, the lighthouse is open to the public for guided tours. A tour of this 65-foot tall structure, however, is not for the faint of heart. It involves climbing 57 steps of a spiral staircase inside the lighthouse and climbing an eight-rung ladder into the light room. The payoff is huge when you experience the amazing view from atop the light.

Biloxi Mississippi Lighthouse

1050 Beach Blvd (U.S. 90) • Biloxi, Mississippi 39530
(228) 374-3105 • www.biloxi.ms.us

Spotted Sea Trout with Sriracha Lime Mayonnaise

Spotted sea trout from the Gulf of Mexico are also commonly referred to as speckled trout and yellowmouth trout. There's a good chance your fishing guide might just call them "specks" or "yellers." As with most seafood, "specks" and "yellers" hold the most flavor when cooked fresh.

4 skinless spotted sea trout fillets
Lemon juice
2 eggs, lightly beaten
2 tablespoons beer
1 cup panko breadcrumbs
1 teaspoon paprika
1 teaspoon onion powder
¾ teaspoon garlic powder
1 teaspoon black pepper
1 teaspoon salt
Lemon wedges for garnish

Preheat oven to 350°. Lightly drizzle fillets with lemon juice. Mix eggs with beer in a shallow bowl; set aside. In a separate bowl, combine breadcrumbs, paprika, onion powder, garlic powder, pepper and salt. Dip fillets in egg mixture, roll in breadcrumbs and place fillets on a nonstick broiling pan. Turn oven to broil; place pan on middle rack of oven. Broil 4 to 5 minutes. Turn gently, and broil an additional 4 to 5 minutes until crust is golden brown. Fish is done when it flakes. Serve hot with Sriracha Lime Mayonnaise. Garnish with lemon wedges.

Sriracha Lime Mayonnaise:

½ cup mayonnaise
1½ tablespoons Sriracha hot sauce
½ tablespoon lime juice
½ teaspoon sugar

Combine mayonnaise, hot sauce, lime juice and sugar; mix well.

Biloxi Beer-Battered Hot Fish Fillets

I ate hot fish for the first time in Biloxi, Mississippi, during a college trip. I have always liked food with a little burn to it.

Batter:

2 cups self-rising flour
1 (12-ounce) bottle beer
1½ tablespoons Cajun seasoning
Garlic powder, salt and pepper to taste

In a large bowl, mix flour and beer until a batter is formed. Add seasonings and mix well.

Fish:

6 to 8 fresh white fish fillets
Cajun seasoning
Flour for dusting
Oil for frying

Season both sides of each fillet with Cajun seasoning; dust with flour. Heat oil in deep fryer to 350°. Dip each piece of flour-dusted fish in batter to coat evenly; place in fryer. Cook a few pieces at a time, so hot oil reaches every piece. Allow oil to regain its heat between batches. Cook until golden brown. Serve immediately.

Blackened Fish

Oil for frying
2 to 4 white fish fillets

Heat oil in an oven-safe skillet over medium-high heat. Dredge fillets in Blackening Seafood Seasoning Mix. Carefully place in hot skillet and cook just long enough to sear the outside. Place skillet in 325° oven and bake just until fish flakes easily, 8 to 10 minutes. Top with a bit more seasoning before serving.

Blackening Seafood Seasoning Mix:

2 teaspoons salt
2 teaspoons paprika
2 teaspoons onion powder
1½ teaspoons seafood seasoning
1 teaspoon garlic powder
1 teaspoon black pepper
1 teaspoon cayenne pepper
½ teaspoon oregano

Mix all ingredients together; store covered in a cool, dry place until ready to use.

Cedar Plank Grilled Cobia

Cobia is very tender with a rich sweet flavor. Making the fillets perfect for cedar plank grilling.

4 cobia fillets
1½ tablespoons olive oil
½ teaspoon seafood seasoning
1 tablespoon lemon juice
½ tablespoon chopped basil

2 teaspoons thyme
1 teaspoon pepper
Dash salt
4 untreated cedar planks, soaked

Rinse fillets and pat dry. Place in a glass baking dish; top with a light drizzle of olive oil and sprinkle with seafood seasoning. Drizzle with lemon juice then season with basil, thyme, pepper and salt. Cover and chill while soaking the cedar planks. Place planks in water using a weight—brick wrapped in aluminum foil, for example—to completely submerge. Set aside to soak 1 to 2 hours or longer. Halfway through, flip planks to ensure equal soaking.

Preheat grill to medium-high heat. Place fillets on cedar planks; place on grill at same time. (During cooking, you may notice the cedar plank flaming up. The flames help to get the plank smoldering to produce the sweet cedar smoke. Spray just enough water directly on the flames to extinguish them. You don't want to stop the plank from smoldering.) Close lid and cook 10 minutes. Open grill and rotate planks to ensure even cooking. (Do not flip fish.) Close lid and grill another 8 to 10 minutes or until fillets have golden brown edges and flake easily.

Creole Baked Redfish with Tangy Chili Mayo

Many Gulf of Mexico residents refer to redfish simply as "reds.". Whatever you call them, redfish fillets are perfect for a wide variety of recipes. Fresh-from-the-gulf fillets are easy to handle and boast a subtle mild flavor with a touch of sweetness.

4 to 6 redfish fillets, rinsed and paper towel dried
Olive oil
Lemon juice
Creole or Cajun seasoning

Preheat oven to 375°. Drizzle both sides of fillets with a small amount of olive oil and lemon juice; sprinkle both sides with Creole seasoning. Place in a treated glass baking dish; bake 10 minutes. If fillets flake easily, remove from oven; if not, cook another 5 minutes or just until fish flakes easily. Serve with Tangy Chili Mayo on the side. These yummy redfish are perfect served over steamed vegetables, rice or pasta.

Tangy Chili Mayo:

½ cup mayonnaise
2 tablespoons sour cream
1 tablespoon water
Juice of 1 lime

1 tablespoon chili sauce (taco sauce is
a great substitution)
3 teaspoons chili powder
Salt and pepper to taste

In a glass bowl, mix all ingredients; cover. Chill before using.

Crunchy Grilled Snapper Burritos with Avocado Mayo

Avocado Mayo:

1 ripe avocado, peeled and pit removed
¼ cup sour cream
2 tablespoons mayonnaise
½ teaspoon salt

Mash avocado in a bowl; add sour cream, mayonnaise and salt. Cover and chill until needed.

Crunchy Cabbage Filling:

3 cups cabbage slaw mix
½ cup diced tomato
¼ cup chopped fresh cilantro
2 tablespoons lime juice
¾ tablespoon finely chopped jalapeño
3 teaspoons minced garlic
Salt and pepper to taste

In a bowl, combine slaw mix, tomatoes, cilantro, lime juice, jalapeño and garlic. Mix. Add salt and pepper to taste. Toss again to evenly mix.

Snapper Fillets:

6 (6-ounce) boneless skinless snapper fillets
1 tablespoon olive oil
3 tablespoons Coastal Tex-Mex Seasoning Mix (page 161)
6 (10-inch) flour tortillas

Preheat grill. Lightly coat fillets with oil and sprinkle each with ½ tablespoon seasoning mix. Lightly grease grilling basket, foil sheets or the grill grates. Grill fillets 2 to 3 minutes on one side; turn and grill other side an additional 2 to 3 minutes or until fillets will flake easily with a fork when done. Spread Avocado Mayo over each tortilla, add a layer of Crunchy Cabbage Filling down the center and top with a hot fillet. Fold ends of tortilla; roll up tightly. Serve hot.

Baked Chili Lime Wahoo Tostados

3 tablespoons soy sauce
2 tablespoons fresh lime juice
1 tablespoon minced garlic
2 teaspoons chili powder
1 teaspoon red pepper flakes
1 tablespoon butter
4 wahoo fillets, skinless
8 corn tostado shells
1 cup spring mix lettuce
1 avocado, peeled and chopped
1 cup diced tomato
1 cup crumbled fresco cheese
Chili sauce (or taco sauce)

Preheat oven to 350°. In a saucepan over low heat, cook soy sauce, lime juice, garlic, chili powder, red pepper flakes and butter until butter melts. Arrange fillets in a glass baking dish; evenly coat with sauce, making sure to get both sides. Bake 25 minutes or until edges are slightly golden. Arrange tostado shells on a cookie sheet; lightly warm in oven, for 1 to 2 minutes. Remove fillets from oven and break into big chunks. Top shells with lettuce, avocado, tomato, cheese and wahoo. Lightly drizzle with chili sauce.

Fort Massachusetts

Fort Massachusetts is located on Ship Island about an hour's boat ride off the coast of Mississippi making getting there half the fun. Construction of the "Fort on Ship Island"—as referenced in historical records because it was never officially named—began in 1859 and wasn't complete when Mississippi seceded from the Union in January 1961. During the Civil War, the island was taken by Confederate militia who soon abandoned it due to the harsh environment. Official Confederate troops returned soon after. On July 9th, the Union Navy's USS Massachusetts came within range of cannons mounted by Confederate troops. The 20-minute skirmish, which resulted in very few injuries and little damage to either side, was the only military engagement that would directly involve the fort. Union Troops occupied the island and the fort in the spring of 1861. Seeing the fort now, it's hard to imagine 60 warships anchored just off shore while up to 18000 troops practiced maneuvers for an eminent coming battle. Today, the fort sits quietly at the end of West Ship Island and fun for families to explore.

Fort Massachusetts

Ship Island • Gulfport, Mississippi 39530
(228) 230-4100 • www.nps.gov/guis

Photo courtesy Mike Kennedy, travel writer for the New Orleans based travel blog NOadventure.com

Spicy Shrimp Tacos with Easy Texas Tartar Sauce

2 pounds large shrimp, peeled and deveined
4 tablespoons butter
3 tablespoons beer
½ teaspoon minced garlic
1 (1.25-ounce) envelope taco seasoning, divided
Soft flour tortillas
Toppings

Rinse shrimp; drain. In a skillet, sauté shrimp in butter and beer. Season with garlic and three quarters of the taco seasoning. Stir to coat shrimp; cook 6 minutes. Add remaining taco seasoning and toss to evenly coat. Serve on soft flour taco shells with your choice of toppings and drizzled with Easy Texas Tartar Sauce.

Easy Texas Tartar Sauce:

1 cup mayonnaise
3 tablespoons relish
½ tablespoon minced jalapeño
2 to 3 teaspoons lime juice

Combine all and stir to mix well.

Fish Tacos

4 cups baked or broiled grouper
Cajun seasoning to taste
1 cup shredded cabbage
1 cup shredded lettuce
1 cup prepared salsa
Dash cumin powder
Salt and pepper, to taste
8 medium-size tortillas
Shredded Cheddar cheese

Flake fish; season to taste with Cajun seasoning. Set aside. Combine cabbage, lettuce and salsa. Add cumin, salt and pepper; mix well. Place ½ cup fish in a tortilla; top with cabbage mixture and cheese. Serve with sour cream or tartar sauce.

Jerk Rubbed Black Drum with Easy Black Beans and Rice

Pick the freshest Gulf of Mexico black drum fillets you can find and get ready for some Caribbean-style flavor.

⅓ cup lime juice
2 tablespoons jerk or spicy Caribbean-style rub
2 tablespoons olive oil
1 tablespoon minced garlic
4 boneless skinless black drum fillets
1 (12-ounce) box seasoned yellow rice mix
1 (10-ounce) can spicy diced tomatoes with green chiles
1 cup frozen peas and carrots
2 (15-ounce) cans black beans, drained
⅓ cup finely chopped onion

In a bowl, combine lime juice, jerk seasoning, olive oil and garlic; mix well. Spread over fillets in a glass baking dish. Cover and chill 30 minutes to an hour. Preheat oven to 350°. Prepare yellow rice mix as directed on packaging. Before removing from heat, add tomatoes and chiles, peas and carrots, black beans and onion. Simmer until excess liquid cooks off. Bake fillets 15 to 20 minutes or until flakes easily. Serve hot with a side of black beans and rice.

Lemon Pepper Amberjack

4 amberjack fillets
1 (6-ounce) container lime yogurt
2 lemons, divided
Salt and pepper to taste
Parsley to taste
Oregano to taste
1 tablespoon butter, melted
½ cup sliced almonds, toasted

Marinate fillets in yogurt 30 minutes. Top with juice of 1 lemon; sprinkle with salt, black pepper, parsley and oregano. Bake 20 minutes at 350° or until fish flakes. Top fish with a squeeze of lemon juice, butter and almonds. Delicious served with a side of Cajun-style dirty rice.

Grilled Amberjack Fillets with Toasted Corn and Black Bean Salsa

Toasted Corn and Black Bean Salsa:

1 (15-ounce) can whole-kernel corn, drained
1 (15-ounce) can black beans, drained and rinsed
1½ cups chopped tomatoes
½ cup diced red onion
1 tablespoon chopped jalapeño
½ tablespoon chopped cilantro
2 teaspoons chili powder
Salt and pepper to taste
1 tablespoon lime juice

Place corn on nonstick cookie sheet; broil in oven until corn starts to brown. Toss gently with a spatula; return to oven. Continue to broil until edges are golden and browned. Combine with remaining ingredients in glass bowl; mix. Cover and chill 1 hour or longer before serving.

Fillets:

4 amberjack fillets
1 stick butter, melted
½ tablespoon cumin powder
2 to 3 teaspoons chili powder
3 teaspoons lemon juice
Black pepper to taste

Place fillets in a glass baking dish; brush with melted butter and sprinkle with seasonings. Turn fillets over; repeat. Let rest about 20 minutes as grill preheats. Use a grilling basket or tray coated with nonstick spray; grill over medium-high heat 3 to 4 minutes per side or until fish flakes. Serve hot, topped with Toasted Corn and Black Bean Salsa.

Whiskey Glazed Cast-Iron Amberjack Fillets

Don't worry if you don't have a cast-iron skillet for this recipe. A nice hot skillet will work fine. The cast-iron just gives a more rustic flavor and feel.

4 (6- to 7-ounce) amberjack fillets
¼ cup whiskey or bourbon
2 tablespoons soy sauce
1 tablespoon water
1 tablespoon lime juice
3 tablespoons brown sugar
½ tablespoon ginger powder
1 tablespoon minced garlic
½ teaspoon black pepper
½ teaspoon chili powder
Butter for frying

Place fillets in a glass baking dish. In a bowl, combine whiskey, soy sauce, water, lime juice, brown sugar, ginger powder, garlic, pepper and chili powder; mix until spices dissolve. Spread evenly over fillets, turning to coat both sides. Cover; refrigerate 1 hour. Heat a large cast-iron skillet over medium-high heat; add 3 tablespoons butter. Carefully add fillets to skillet; fry 2 to 3 minutes each side turning once. Don't let your skillet get too hot. Add more butter as needed.

Seared Coconut Rum Grouper

I love grouper! This is one of my favorite recipes.

4 grouper fillets, about ¾ inch thick
Seafood seasoning to taste
Creole seasoning to taste
Oil for pan cooking

Coconut Rum Sauce:

½ stick butter
2 tablespoons soy sauce
2 tablespoons lime juice
2 tablespoons coconut rum
Dash salt and pepper

Rinse grouper fillets and pat dry. Sprinkle with seafood and Creole seasoning and set aside. In a saucepan, prepare Coconut Rum Sauce. Melt butter over medium heat and add remaining ingredients. Stir to mix, reduce heat to low, and simmer while fish cooks. Place grouper fillets in a hot skillet with a bit of oil and cook until edges are golden and fish flakes easily. Drizzle sauce over fillets before removing from heat. Serve remaining sauce on the side or drizzle over fillets when plating.

Baked Pompanos with Pineapple and Mango Salsa

Pompano average around three to four pounds per fish, with some growing upwards to nine pounds. Typically the fillets from pompano run a bit on the small side. This recipe uses two fillets per serving, with four total servings.

Pineapple and Mango Salsa:

½ cup mango, chopped
½ cup pineapple, chopped
1 tablespoon chopped jalapeño
⅓ cup diced red bell pepper

¼ cup diced red onion
½ tablespoon chopped cilantro
⅓ cup orange juice
2 teaspoons Cajun seasoning

In a bowl, combine mango, pineapple, jalapeño, red bell pepper, onion, cilantro, orange juice and Cajun seasoning. Keep at room temperature while fillets are baking.

Fillets:

8 pompano fillets
Olive oil

Dash garlic powder
Dash pepper

Preheat oven to 350°. Place fillets on a nonstick cookie sheet or in a glass baking dish. Drizzle lightly with olive oil; season very lightly with garlic powder and pepper. Bake 15 minutes, or until fish flakes easily. Serve hot, 2 fillets at a time, topped with salsa and your choice of sides.

Wasabi Seared Tuna

6 (6-ounce) tuna steaks
Olive oil

Wasabi Marinade:

1¼ cups white wine
1 cup chopped fresh cilantro leaves
1 cup unsalted butter
¼ cup minced shallots
2 tablespoons white wine vinegar
1 tablespoon wasabi paste
1 tablespoon soy sauce
1 tablespoon olive oil
Salt and pepper to taste

Brush both sides of steaks with olive oil; set aside. In a large bowl, combine Wasabi Marinade ingredients. Add tuna steaks; refrigerate 30 minutes (no longer than 1 hour). In a hot skillet with a bit of oil, sear steaks 2 to 3 minutes per side over high heat. Serve hot.

USS Alabama
Battleship Memorial Park

The USS Alabama (BB-60) served during World War II, earning the name "The Lucky A" because no crew members were lost during combat. The Dakota-class battleship now resides, along with the Gato class submarine USS Drum (SS-228), at Battleship Memorial Park in Mobile Bay. When the USS Alabama was ordered scrapped in 1962, a fundraising effort was started to bring her home to Alabama. School children statewide raised approximately $100,000 in nickels and dimes saved from lunch money and allowances. Battleship Memorial Park is one of the largest tourist attractions in the state. It includes a world-class military aviation museum, outdoor static displays and memorials, as well as a gift shop and diner. Both the Alabama and Drum are open for walking tours.

USS Alabama
Battleship Memorial Park

2703 Battleship Parkway • Mobile, Alabama 36602
(251) 433-2703 • www.ussalabama.com

Thai Swordfish Steaks with Five Spice Quinoa

Swordfish Steaks:

½ cup light brown sugar
½ cup soy sauce
¼ cup ketchup
2 or 3 green onions, thinly sliced

1 teaspoon ginger
1 teaspoon minced garlic
4 swordfish steaks

In a medium bowl, combine sugar, soy sauce, ketchup, onions, ginger and garlic; mix well. Place steaks in glass baking dish; evenly coat with marinade. Cover; chill 2 to 3 hours. Preheat grill to medium-high heat; remove steaks from marinade and grill each side 4 to 5 minutes. The steak will flake easily with a fork when done. Serve hot with a serving of Five Spice Quinoa.

Five Spice Quinoa:

1½ teaspoons ground cinnamon
1½ teaspoons ground anise
½ teaspoon ground fennel seed
½ teaspoon black pepper

¼ teaspoon ground clove
1 (16-ounce) box quinoa, easy/quick
  cooking style
2 to 3 teaspoons soy sauce

Combine the five spices in a small bowl; stir to mix. Prepare quinoa as directed on the package. When quinoa comes to a boil, add spices and soy sauce.

Coastal Fried Catfish

Somewhere along the line where fresh water and salt water meet is the boundary where good old-fashioned southern-style catfish comes to an end.

4 catfish fillets (or 8 to 10 catfish nuggets)
1 egg
4 tablespoons butter, melted
¾ cup all-purpose flour
½ teaspoon salt
½ teaspoon pepper
½ teaspoon garlic powder
Oil
2 tablespoons parsley flakes
Lemon juice

Clean and rinse catfish. In a bowl, whisk egg and butter; set aside. In another bowl, combine flour, salt, pepper and garlic powder. Dip fish into egg mixture then flour mixture; fry in hot oil until fish rises to the top and turns golden brown. Sprinkle parsley over fish. Serve hot with a squirt of lemon juice.

Gulf Coast Classic Fish and Seasoned Chips

Nothing beats a nice serving of fish and chips when visiting the Gulf Coast. With this recipe you can have them anytime. Start the chips first and keep them warm in the oven while cooking the fish.

Seasoned Chips:

4 large russet potatoes
Oil for frying
Garlic powder, salt and cinnamon to taste

Preheat oven to 200°. Place a wire rack on a cookie sheet with sides. Cut potatoes into fries or chips, skin on; soak in cold water while oil heats. Drain fries well before frying. Fry in small batches, turning as needed. When golden brown, remove to prepared wire rack. Place in warm oven while cooking fish.

Fish:

6 to 8 boneless fish fillets, halved lengthwise
Cornstarch or flour, for dredging
2 cups all-purpose flour
1 tablespoon baking powder
1 teaspoon salt
1 teaspoon black pepper
½ teaspoon seafood seasoning
1 (12-ounce) bottle dark beer

Dredge fish in flour or cornstarch, shaking off excess; set aside. Combine 2 cups flour and remaining ingredients in a bowl to make a batter. Ensure oil is heated between 350° and 375°. Dip fish into batter; place in hot oil. When fillets rise to the top, rotate them for even cooking. Cook until batter is golden brown.

Oven Fried Grouper Fillets with Seasoned Baked Chips

This recipe is perfect for grouper fillets but you can substitute your choice of fresh Gulf of Mexico seafood. Go ahead and cook the chips first and let them cool and crisp while you prepare the fillets. You can also halve the fillets for easy handling.

Baked Chips:

4 medium baking potatoes, peeled
Water for blanching
1½ tablespoons olive oil
Salt and pepper to taste
2 to 3 teaspoons Cajun seasoning

Preheat oven to 450°. Slice peeled potatoes into ⅛-inch thick round slices. (Try to keep them all the same thickness for even baking.) Put enough water in a saucepan to cover potatoes; bring to a boil, cooking 3 to 4 minutes. Quickly drain; place in a bowl. Gently toss with olive oil, salt, pepper and Cajun seasoning. Toss to coat evenly; place potatoes in a single layer on a cookie sheet treated with nonstick spray. Bake 15 minutes until crisp and golden brown. Gently remove chips, place on a rack to cool, and sprinkle with Cajun seasoning.

Grouper:

1 large egg, beaten
¼ cup flour
½ teaspoon cayenne pepper
½ teaspoon salt
4 cups cornflakes cereal, crushed
4 to 6 grouper fillets

When chips are done, decrease oven to 425°. Place egg in a shallow bowl. Add flour to another bowl. In a larger third bowl, combine cayenne pepper, salt and crushed cereal. Gently dust each fillet with flour, dip into egg and gently roll in crushed cereal, coating completely. Arrange in a single layer on a treated cookie sheet with sides. Lightly spray cereal coating with nonstick spray. Bake 18 to 20 minutes until golden brown and fillets flake easily with a fork.

Seaside Fish Tenders

This recipe is a bit spicy. It has the flavor of a jerk chicken with a distinct citrus-flavored punch. Select thicker whole fillets and cut lengthwise for tenders. This recipe is delicious made with chicken tenders, too.

½ cup pineapple juice
½ cup orange juice
1 tablespoon minced garlic
⅓ cup minced onion
⅓ cup hot sauce

1 tablespoon cumin powder
2 tablespoons chili powder
Salt and pepper to taste
20 fish fillets, halved length-wise

In a glass baking dish, combine juices, garlic, onion, hot sauce, cumin, chili powder, salt and pepper; add fish and turn to coat. Cover; refrigerate at least 1 hour. Grill over medium-high heat until fish flakes easily with a fork.

Batter Version:

1½ cups self-rising flour
1½ cups beer
Salt and pepper to taste
Breadcrumbs
Oil for frying

Combine flour, beer, salt and pepper to make batter. Dip fish in batter; roll in breadcrumbs. Fry in deep fryer at 350° for 3 to 5 minutes until golden brown.

Southern Fried Hot Fish with Cornbread Salad

Fried hot fish is a staple at just about any good southern fish fry. Start with the cornbread salad, as it needs time to chill before serving.

Cornbread Salad:

1 (8.5-ounce) box Jiffy cornbread mix, plus ingredients to prepare
1 cup diced onion
1 bell pepper, seeded and diced
1 cup diced tomatoes
1 (15-ounce) can whole-kernel corn, drained
1 (15-ounce) can pinto beans, rinsed
½ cup real bacon bits
1½ cups shredded Cheddar cheese
2 cups mayonnaise

Bake cornbread according to package directions. Allow to cool; crumble over a large bowl into big pieces. (Don't make them too small since they will continue to break up as you mix.) Add remaining ingredients; mix gently. Chill before serving.

Southern Fried Hot Fish

1½ pounds fresh flounder fillets
1½ cups buttermilk
1 tablespoon hot sauce
½ tablespoon Cajun seasoning
1½ cups cornmeal
1½ cups all-purpose flour
1½ teaspoons baking powder
1½ teaspoons salt
1 tablespoon Cajun seasoning
Oil for frying

Place fillets in a deep bowl. In another bowl, combine buttermilk, hot sauce and Cajun seasoning; pour over fillets, lifting fillets to coat evenly. Sprinkle more seasoning on top, if desired. Set aside 30 minutes to marinate.

In a bowl, combine cornmeal, flour, baking powder, salt and Cajun seasoning. Roll each fillet in flour and cornmeal mixture, coating completely. Fry in 375° oil, turning as needed, 3 to 5 minutes until golden brown. Remove from oil; cool slightly on a rack. Serve hot with Cornbread Salad on the side.

A Dozen Raw Oysters on the Half Shell

Ally loves oysters. Here is her simple tried-and-true method for enjoying a few on the half shell.

12 fresh oysters in the shell
12 saltine crackers
Ally's Homemade Cocktail Sauce (page 150)

Scrub oysters under cold running water to remove grit and sand paying special attention to the hinge area where grit has a tendency to settle. (If you have time, place oysters in ice for about an hour so they will be chilled when serving.) To shuck, use a durable, thick cloth and fold it over several times to protect your hand and steady the oyster. Place an oyster, cup-side down in the palm of your towel-covered hand with hinge facing you. Insert the tip of an oyster knife (or dull butter knife) carefully into hinge. (Don't jab or apply too much pressure to prevent breaking the shell.) Applying gentle pressure, twist knife back and forth to pry shell open. Cut oyster away from top shell. Bend shell back to release it and discard that top shell. Run knife under oyster to release it from bottom shell; work carefully to reserve as much liquid as possible. To eat, place meat on a cracker and top with Ally's Homemade Cocktail Sauce. If serving guests or for a family dinner, place oyster in the shell on a bed of crushed ice with a bowl of Ally's Homemade Cocktail Sauce in the center.

Fried Apalachicola Oysters

The trick to frying oysters is having your oil at the right temperature and not overcooking them. Cooking time should range around two to three minutes. This same breading mixture also works well with shrimp, okra, jalapeño slices, fish and more.

12 Apalachicola oysters, shucked
⅓ cup milk
⅔ cup all-purpose flour
½ cup crushed corn chips or breadcrumbs
½ teaspoon salt
¼ teaspoon pepper
Dash Tabasco sauce
Oil for pan frying

Drain liquid from oysters, removing shell pieces. Rinse with cold water, place in a bowl, and cover with 1/3 cup milk. In a separate bowl, combine flour, corn chips, salt and pepper; mix. Working one oyster at time, remove from milk, dash with Tabasco, and roll in breading to coat completely. Drop oysters into hot oil, working batches to not overcrowd the oil. Fry 2 to 3 minutes or until golden brown. Drain on absorbent paper. Serve hot.

Gulf Coast Oysters Rockefeller

Oysters Rockefeller was created at the New Orleans restaurant, Antoine's, which was founded in 1840. Jules Alciatore, son of the restaurant's founder, created his now famous oyster dish in 1899.

2 dozen Gulf Coast oysters, shucked on the half shell
2 cups cooked and drained spinach
⅓ cup chopped celery
¼ cup chopped onion
2 fresh bay leaves
1 teaspoon chopped parsley
½ teaspoon minced garlic
⅓ cup butter
¼ teaspoon hot pepper sauce
Salt and pepper to taste
½ cup dry breadcrumbs
1 tablespoon lemon juice

Place oysters in a baking dish. Combine spinach, celery, onion, bay leaves, parsley and garlic in a food processor blending until smooth. Pour into a saucepan over medium heat. Add butter, hot sauce, salt and pepper. Cook until butter is melted and ingredients are well combined. Remove from heat and stir in breadcrumbs and lemon juice; mix well. Spoon over oysters. Bake at 400° until oyster edges curl. Serve hot.

Dry Tortugas National Park

Fort Jefferson is found one of the 7 islands of Dry Tortugas National Park just under 70 miles west of Key West in the Gulf of Mexico. Around 60,000 people a year travel to the remote location by ferry, private boat, charter boat, or seaplane. Jaun Ponce de León visited the area in 1513 capturing over 160 sea turtles referring to the islands as the "Tortugas." The term "Dry" refers to the lack of freshwater. Fort Jeffersona massive, unfinished coastal fort became a prisoner camp following the Civil War once housing Dr. Samuel Mudd who was convicted of aiding President Lincoln assassin John Wilkes Booth. A favorite fishing spot of Ernest Hemingway when he lived in Key West, the island has also been a frequent landing spot for Cuban refugees. A visit to the park can include swimming, snorkeling, camping and more but should also include plenty of planning as there is no fuel, charcoal, water or food service available. There is a small gift shop and tours are conducted by the staff of Everglades National Park.

Dry Tortugas National Park

40001 SR-9336 • Homestead, Florida 33034

(305) 242-7700 • www.nps.gov/drto

Baked Gulf Clams with White Wine Butter Sauce and Rustic Potatoes

A clam bake can take place on the beach, the patio, or even in the kitchen.

Rustic Potatoes:

2 pounds red or gold new potatoes, halved
Salt to taste
¼ cup olive oil
2 tablespoons chopped green onion
½ tablespoon oregano
½ tablespoon parsley
½ tablespoon minced garlic
2 teaspoons thyme
Salt and pepper to taste

Preheat oven to 400°. Place potatoes in a stockpot with water to cover; salt to taste. Bring to a boil; cook 4 to 5 minutes until potatoes are soft, but not mushy. Remove from heat, drain and place in a large bowl. Add olive oil, green onion, oregano, parsley, garlic, thyme, salt and pepper. Gently toss to coat. Spread potatoes in a single layer on a treated baking sheet. Set aside while preparing clams.

Clams and Butter Sauce:

4 dozen clams, rinsed well
4 tablespoons butter
2 tablespoons olive oil
½ cup white wine
3 cloves minced garlic
2 tablespoons parsley
½ teaspoon oregano

Rinse clams, discarding any that have already opened. Arrange clams in a glass baking dish. Place clams and potatoes in oven. Reduce heat to 350°; bake 10 minutes. While clams and potatoes are baking, melt butter in a saucepan. Add olive oil, wine, garlic, parsley and oregano. Simmer until clams and potatoes are done. At 10 minutes bake time, check clams. If all are not open, cook another 2 minutes. Check potatoes; if they are cooked through remove from oven. At 12 minutes cook time, remove everything from oven. Discard any clams that did not open. Spoon butter sauce over clams and serve hot with Rustic Potatoes on the side.

Shrimp Naan Bread Pizza with Ricotta Sauce

If you can't find naan bread at your local grocery store, feel free to substitute your favorite flat bread or pizza crust.

4 tablespoons butter
1 pound large shrimp, peeled and
   deveined
1 tablespoon minced garlic
½ tablespoon Italian seasoning
½ tablespoon lemon juice
½ cup ricotta cheese
2 to 3 tablespoons milk, divided
⅓ cup shredded Parmesan cheese

¼ cup finely chopped onion
1 tablespoon Italian seasoning
Dash parsley flakes
2 (8-to 10-inch) pieces naan bread
½ cup spinach, stems removed
⅓ cup julienne-cut tomato (oven
   roasted if desired)
1½ cups shredded mozzarella
   cheese

Preheat oven to 300°. Melt butter in a small skillet; add shrimp, garlic, Italian seasoning and lemon juice. Sauté shrimp until just cooked through and slightly browned. (Don't overcook, as they will continue to cook in the oven.) Remove from heat; set aside. For sauce, combine ricotta cheese, Parmesan cheese, 2 tablespoons milk, onion, Italian seasoning and parsley in a saucepan over medium heat. Cook, stirring, until cheese is melted; use additional milk, if needed. Spread sauce over naan bread; top with spinach, tomato and shrimp. Spread mozzarella cheese over all. Bake on a cookie sheet 10 minutes or until cheese is melted and bubbly.

Shrimp and Veggie Pizza

This version of a cream cheese summer pizza combines fresh veggies with the flavor of Gulf of Mexico shrimp. You can also use crabmeat, bay scallops, or flaked fish. Bake the crust, allow it to cool, then start adding your toppings. The trick for a delicious shrimp and veggie pizza is using completely cooked and cooled seafood and allowing all your vegetables to completely drain and dry after you rinse and cut them. This keeps any added moisture from seeping out of the vegetables.

2½ cups small to medium shrimp (cooked, shelled, tails removed and deveined)
2 (8-ounce) packages crescent dough sheets
1 cup sour cream
1 (8-ounce) package cream cheese, softened
1 teaspoon dried dill weed
1 teaspoon garlic salt

1 (1-ounce) package dry ranch dressing mix
Dash pepper
1 cup thinly sliced radishes
1 red bell pepper, diced
2 cups chopped broccoli
1 cup grated carrots
½ cup diced tomato, drained on a paper towel

Preheat oven per directions on crescent roll package; spray a cookie or pizza pan with nonstick spray. Press dough into pan, forming to its shape. Use a fork to poke a bunch of holes in dough, to prevent bubbles; bake 9 to 10 minutes. Remove from oven; cool completely. In a bowl, combine sour cream, cream cheese, dill weed, garlic salt, ranch mix and pepper; spread over crust leaving a little room on the edges. Spread shrimp and vegetables over top. Refrigerate 30 minutes or until ready to serve.

Easy Bayou-Style Boiled Shrimp

This recipe is one step away from a Cajun Shrimp Boil. Add seafood seasoning, corn on the cob, whole new potatoes and thick slices of smoked sausage plus more water to cover and there you are.

2 pounds fresh shrimp
4 quarts water
½ onion, diced
½ green bell pepper, sliced
2 (5-ounce) bottles Tabasco sauce
2 teaspoons black pepper
1 tablespoon butter
1 tablespoon celery salt

Rinse shrimp; set aside. In a large stockpot, bring water and remaining ingredients to a boil. Add shrimp; boil 10 minutes.

Foil Pack Shrimp Boil

This is another take on the classic shrimp boil. This time in a miniature versions straight off the grill. I suggest using heavy-duty foil or small foil pans with foil lids when making Fail Pack Shrimp Boil.

4 ears corn, husked and halved
8 small red potatoes
1 pound medium shrimp, peeled and deveined
2 cups sliced smoked sausage, 1-inch pieces
1 red bell pepper, sliced
3½ tablespoons olive oil
2 teaspoons minced garlic
½ tablespoon seafood seasoning
½ tablespoon chili powder
Salt and pepper to taste

The secret to this recipe is a bit of precooking. Boil potatoes and corn in salted water to cover 15 minutes. Lay out 4 10-inch square sheets of heavy-duty aluminum foil. Place 1 piece of corn and 2 potatoes on each sheet. Divide shrimp, sausage and bell pepper between each. Drizzle with olive oil; sprinkle with garlic, seafood seasoning, chili powder, salt and pepper. Fold foil from all four sides to seal tightly. Grill over medium heat 20 minutes or until shrimp are done and potatoes are tender.

Palm Harbor Garlic Shrimp

My good friend Crystal and I enjoyed some delicious garlic shrimp on a trip to Tampa Bay. My Palm Harbor Garlic Shrimp includes a bit of ginger for an interesting twist.

⅓ cup olive oil
1 pound jumbo shrimp, cooked
1 tablespoon minced garlic
1 (4-ounce) can chopped green chiles
¼ teaspoon freshly grated ginger
Salt and pepper to taste
Parsley flakes for garnish
Lemon

Heat oil in a large skillet over medium-high heat. Add shrimp and saute 3 minutes. Add garlic, green chiles, ginger, salt and pepper; continue to cook another 2 to 3 minutes or until shrimp turn pink. Remove to a serving dish and garnish with parsley. Finish with a squeeze of lemon.

Fort Morgan State Historical Site

Fort Morgan, located on the Alabama Gulf Coast at the mouth of Mobile Bay, shared Civil War duty with Fort Gaines just across the mouth of the bay on Dauphin Island. Construction of Fort Morgan began in 1819 following the War of 1812. It took fifteen years for completion. Slave labor was responsible for building the fort, using 30,000,000 handmade bricks. At the outset of World War I, the fort was called back into action, and during the Depression, President Franklin Roosevelt's Works Project Administration included the fort in projects designed to put people back to work. Fort Morgan was again brought back into service for World War II in 1941–1944, serving to protect the coastline and stand watch for German U-boats. It's easy to see the fort's modifications during 100 years of use with changing artillery and technology. Fort Morgan is now under the management of the State of Alabama and the Alabama Historical Commission. The site includes the fort, a museum, public areas, and historical grounds with artillery batteries.

Fort Morgan State Historical Site

110 State Highway 180 • Gulf Shores, Alabama 36542

(251) 540-7127 • www.fort-morgan.org

Shrimp and Cheese Grits

2 tablespoons butter
1 tablespoon minced garlic
2 scallions, chopped
1 cup spinach
2 teaspoons thyme
1 cup quick cooking grits
3½ cups low-sodium chicken broth
1 cup low-fat plain yogurt
½ teaspoon salt
½ teaspoon freshly ground black pepper
2 teaspoons hot sauce
2 cups small peeled shrimp
1 cup shredded Cheddar cheese

Melt butter in large saucepan; add garlic, scallions, spinach and thyme. Cook 2 minutes. Add grits; cook 2 more minutes, stirring constantly. Whisk in broth. Add yogurt and whisk well. Add salt, pepper and hot sauce; simmer 6 minutes. Add shrimp and cheese; cook 8 minutes. Cover, remove from heat, and let sit, covered, for 5 minutes before serving.

Creole Shrimp and Biscuits

Don't let the fact that a biscuit is included in this simple recipe lead you to believe that shrimp and biscuits are only for breakfast. This dish can be enjoyed anytime of the day.

1 pound medium shrimp, peeled and deveined
Creole seasoning
1 (12-ounce) can flaky-style biscuits
1 small onion, diced
½ tablespoon minced garlic
1 (14-ounce) can chicken broth
1 cup heavy cream
1 tablespoon flour

6 slices thick-cut bacon, cooked and crumbled
1 cup shredded sharp Cheddar cheese
2 teaspoons garlic powder
2 teaspoons onion powder
2 teaspoons hot sauce
1 teaspoon black pepper
½ teaspoon salt

Rinse shrimp; season to taste with Creole seasoning. Cook biscuits according to directions on package. While biscuits cook, place a large skillet over medium-high heat. Add onion and garlic; cook until onion start to brown. Add chicken broth and shrimp; cook 8 minutes to reduce slightly. Reduce heat to simmer; stir in cream and flour to thicken. Turn off heat; add bacon, cheese, and Creole seasoning to taste. Stir in garlic powder, onion powder, hot sauce, pepper and salt. Stir to mix well. Serve hot in a bowl with a biscuit on top, or serve the biscuit open-faced topped Creole Shrimp.

Macee's Battered Popcorn Shrimp

Our son loves popcorn shrimp. He actually loves shrimp in general. Here is a simple way to make popcorn shrimp that has more flavor than what you can generally find on a starter menu. This shrimp is perfect for serving in a po'boy sandwich.

1½ pounds headless shrimp, peeled and cleaned
1½ cup all-purpose flour, divided
1 cup cornmeal
1 cup beer
¼ cup sugar
1 egg, beaten
2 tablespoons Cajun seasoning
¼ cup minced onion
1 tablespoon garlic powder

Rinse shrimp; set aside. Mix 1 cup flour and remaining ingredients to make a batter. Place remaining ½ cup flour in a shallow bowl. Dredge shrimp in flour and gently dip in batter. Working in batches, fry several shrimp at a time in hot oil until golden brown. Drain on a paper towel or wire rack. Sprinkle with additional Cajun seasoning, if desired. Serve hot.

About Cooking and Cleaning Crabs

There are so many ways to cook crab. Cook them in the shell, shelled, boiled, baked, or even fried. But, in general, most crab recipes call for whole live crab. To cook a live crab, simply boil, steam, or fry per the recipe. To kill a crab before cooking, puncture shell between the eyes using a knife. To clean, lay dead crab on its back. Remove the apron and gills, clip off eyes, mouth, and feelers. Rinse well and use as described in recipe.

How to Boil Blue Crabs

Fill a big, sturdy pot with enough water (estimated) to cover crabs). Place over high heat, cover and bring water to a rolling boil. When water is boiling, drop crabs into the pot. (Don't over-crowd them.) Replace lid on pot, and continue to boil over high heat for 10 minutes. Crabs are done when the shells have turned bright orange.

Fried Blue Crabs

Dredging crabs is when you heavily dust the crabs in a flour and cornmeal mixture before frying them. The recipe below is a basic mixture. Feel free to add additional seasoning to make this dish your own.

4 to 6 soft-shell crabs, cleaned and rinsed
½ cup flour
½ cup cornmeal
Salt and pepper to taste
Seafood seasoning to taste
⅔ cup milk
1 egg

Rinse cleaned crabs several times; pat dry with paper towels. Mix flour, cornmeal, salt, pepper and seafood seasoning. In a bowl, combine milk and egg. Dip crabs in egg mixture, dredge heavily in flour mixture to coat evenly and fully, and fry in 350° oil, flipping and turning to cook evenly. Fry 3 to 5 minutes or until golden brown. Serve hot.

Fried Gulf Coast Crabs

6 blue crab
⅓ cup milk
2 eggs, lightly beaten
2½ teaspoons Cajun seasoning
1 teaspoon seafood seasoning
2 cups all-purpose flour
2 teaspoons Cajun seasoning, divided
Vegetable oil for deep frying

Clean crab and rinse several times. In a small bowl, beat milk, egg, seafood seasoning and 1 teaspoon Cajun seasoning. In a separate, shallow bowl, combine flour and remaining 1 teaspoon Cajun seasoning. Dredge crabs in dry flour mixture, then dip in milk mixture and roll crab in flour mixture one more time. Cook crabs in hot oil 2 to 3 minutes. Turn, and fry an additional 2 to 3 minutes until coating is rich golden brown. Remove from oil and drain for a couple of minutes on paper towels. Serve hot.

Stone Crab Claws with Pineapple Sauce

The claws of stone crabs are removed and kept by fishermen and then the crabs are tossed back into the gulf waters where they can regenerate a new claw. Crab claws offer an amazingly sweet flavor that is complemented perfectly with a butter dipping sauce.

2 pounds medium stone crab claws
1 tablespoon lemon juice
1 teaspoon salt
1 cup mayonnaise
2 tablespoons pineapple juice
1 tablespoon spicy mustard
½ tablespoon steak sauce

In a stockpot, bring water to a boil. Add crab claws, lemon juice and salt. Cook 10 minutes. While crab claws are boiling, combine mayonnaise, pineapple juice, spicy mustard and steak sauce in small bowl and refrigerate. Prepare sink or another large pot with ice water. After 10 minutes cook time, remove claws from boiling water using a strainer then submerge in ice water for about 5 minutes. This cools the meat and allows it to pull away from the shell making for easy cracking and eating. Serve Stone Crab Claws with Pineapple Sauce on the side for dipping.

Italian Bay Scallops and Shrimp with Wild Rice

This scallop and shrimp recipe is perfect for a hearty Gulf Coast meal. Plus, it's pretty easy to make.

½ pound bay scallops
½ pound large raw shrimp, peeled and deveined
1 zucchini, chopped into ½-inch pieces
1 red bell pepper, chopped
1 cup quartered red onion
1 cup sliced mushrooms
½ cup chopped carrots
1 cup Italian dressing
1½ cups uncooked wild rice
2 (14-ounce) cans chicken broth
½ tablespoon Italian seasoning
½ cup diced and drained tomato

Rinse and drain scallops and shrimp. Place in a 9x13-inch glass baking dish along with zucchini, bell pepper, onion, mushrooms and carrots. Pour Italian dressing over all, tossing or stirring to evenly coat. Cover and refrigerate while preparing wild rice. Prepare rice per package directions using chicken broth for required liquid (adding additional water, if needed) and including Italian seasoning. Heat grill to medium-high. When rice is almost ready, place seafood and vegetable mixture on a nonstick grilling tray and place on grill. Pour remaining marinade in a microwave-safe bowl, and microwave 5 minutes on high. Baste seafood and vegetables with heated marinade while grilling. Cook until shrimp are opaque and shrimp and scallops have nice golden edges. Stir tomato into mixture just before removing from grill. Serve hot over wild rice.

Florida Lobster Tails

Florida lobster, aka spiny lobster, is found along the gulf and the East Coast from the Caribbean and Brazil, and sometimes as far north as the Carolinas. Unlike New England lobster, Florida lobster does not have claws and has a spiny look.

4 to 6 Florida lobster tails
Melted butter
Tabasco sauce
Lemon juice
Parsley

Split tails with kitchen shears. Coat with butter, a dash of hot sauce, lemon juice and parsley. Cook 10 to 15 minutes in a covered grill over medium high-heat or in a 400° oven. Serve hot.

How to Clarify Butter

For such a simple process, the topic of clarified butter comes up a bunch. If you are wondering how to make clarified butter, just put the amount of butter you want to use in a small saucepan over low heat. Don't stir, poke, mash, or do anything to the butter. When it is completely melted, pour into a see-through glass dish to cool. The butter will begin to separate as it cools. Spoon off the yellow top and discard the clear bottom.

Grilled Zesty Shark Steaks with Easy Pineapple Salsa

Easy Pineapple Salsa:

1 (20-ounce) can pineapple chunks
1 (10-ounce) can diced tomatoes with
   green chiles
2 to 3 green onions (green part only)
   chopped

¼ cup chopped sweet onion
2 tablespoons chopped cilantro
1 lime, juiced
Salt and pepper to taste

In a serving bowl, combine pineapple, tomatoes, onions and cilantro. Drizzle with lime juice; mix well. Season to taste with salt and pepper; set aside for flavors to marry while preparing steak.

Steaks:

4 shark steaks, 1½ inches thick
Salt and pepper to taste
Zesty Italian dressing

Olive oil
Cajun or seafood seasoning

Rub steaks lightly with salt and pepper. Combine pineapple juice with an equal amount Italian dressing; brush generously over steaks. Cover; set aside for 1 hour in refrigerator. Brush grill with olive oil; grill steaks over medium-high heat 3 to 5 minutes each side. When done, season to taste with Cajun or seafood seasoning. Serve topped with Easy Pineapple Salsa.

Crab Coleslaw Salad

4 to 5 cups finely shredded cabbage
2 carrots, shredded
⅓ cup shredded red or green bell pepper
¼ cup minced onion
⅓ cup mayonnaise
¼ cup sour cream
1 tablespoon vinegar
1 teaspoon minced garlic
Salt and pepper to taste
2 teaspoons freshly squeezed lemon juice
½ cup sunflower seeds
1 cup cooked and crumbled crabmeat

In a bowl, combine everything except crabmeat; mix. Add crabmeat, tossing gently to mix.

Creamy Coleslaw

I have been trying slaw recipes for years and this is one of my favorites.

½ head cabbage, shredded
¼ cup chopped celery
¼ cup chopped green bell pepper
¼ cup chopped carrots
½ cup mayonnaise
1½ tablespoons sugar
1 tablespoon vinegar

Mix everything together, cover and cool in refrigerator for 1 hour before serving.

Vinegar-Style Coleslaw

½ head green cabbage, thinly sliced
1 cup thinly sliced red cabbage
2 whole carrots, shredded
3 green onions or scallions, chopped
¼ cup apple cider vinegar
1 tablespoon deli-style mustard (not yellow)
1 tablespoon honey
¼ cup extra virgin olive oil
1½ teaspoons celery seed
Salt and pepper to taste
Toasted sunflower seeds, unsalted (if desired)

In a sealable bowl, combine all ingredients, except sunflower seeds; mix well. Place in refrigerator overnight. Toss lightly with sunflower seeds before serving.

Kent's Cheese Hushpuppies

What could make a hushpuppy better? What could make a hushpuppy better? Cheese and bacon, of course. That's a combination worth trying. For another twist, try adding minced shrimp or crab.

1 cup cornmeal
2 cups self-rising flour
1 cup shredded Cheddar cheese
½ teaspoon salt
⅔ cup milk
1 large egg, beaten
2 tablespoons real bacon bits
½ cup minced onion
⅓ cup butter, melted
Cajun seasoning (optional)

Combine all ingredients except Cajun seasoning in a mixing bowl and mix well. Form into small balls; cook in hot oil until golden brown. As soon as you remove from fryer, sprinkle Cajun seasoning over hushpuppies; serve hot.

Semi Dirty Rice

You will find dirty rice recipes on many menus along the gulf. People love spicy food and this makes a great side dish for many types of seafood.

2 cups brown or wild rice
4 cups water
1 chicken bouillon cube
2 tablespoons hot water
1 pound ground pork sausage
¼ cup chopped jalapeños
½ cup finely chopped red bell pepper
½ cup finely chopped onion
1 tablespoon lemon juice
1 tablespoon Creole seasoning
Large dash salt and pepper

Cook rice with water per package directions. (Wild rice often has a longer cook time than white or brown rice.) In a cup, dissolve bouillon cube in hot water; add to rice. Brown sausage; drain fat. Crumble sausage; stir in remaining ingredients. Combine with cooked rice. Serve hot.

Fort Pike

Louisiana's Fort Pike, named after Brigadier General Zebulon Montgomery Pike, was built following the War of 1812 in 1819. The fort was one of many built during this time period to protect the United States from invasion. Even though the cannons were never fired in battle, the fort has been part of the area's history since completion. During the Seminole Wars, in the 1820's, the fort housed Seminole prisoners prior to their relocation to Oklahoma. The fort switched hands several times during the Civil War and eventually became a training location for former slaves to serve as Union soldiers before being abandoned by the military in 1890. Fort Pike has appeared on TV shows and in movies such as NCIS: New Orleans and G.I. Joe: Retaliation. The park is open by appointment only.

Fort Pike State Historic Site

27100 Chef Menteur Highway • New Orleans, Louisiana 70129
(225) 342-8111

How to Make Flavored Butter

You could use these flavored butters for just about anything, but good seafood needs good butter! Flavored butter is good for about ten days in the fridge or about two months in the freezer. You can mix these in a food processor or in a bowl with a spoon. For great presentation, spoon butter onto a piece of wax paper and roll into a log like premade cookies. Place it in the fridge and allow to firm before slicing to serve.

Cajun Butter

2 sticks butter, softened
2 tablespoons Cajun seasoning
1 teaspoon chili powder
Dash cumin

Combine ingredients. Spoon butter onto wax paper and roll into a log like premade cookies. Refrigerate until firm before slicing.

Lemon Dill Butter

2 sticks butter, softened
2 teaspoons chopped dill weed
2 teaspoons lemon juice
Dash garlic powder

Combine ingredients. Spoon butter onto wax paper and roll into a log like premade cookies. Refrigerate until firm before slicing.

Sweet Honey Butter

2 sticks butter, softened
2 tablespoons honey
1 teaspoon brown sugar
Dash garlic powder

Combine ingredients. Spoon butter onto wax paper and roll into a log like premade cookies. Refrigerate until firm before slicing.

Italian Butter

2 sticks butter, softened
1 tablespoon grated Parmesan cheese
1 teaspoon basil
1 teaspoon parsley flakes
1 teaspoon minced garlic

Combine ingredients. Spoon butter onto wax paper and roll into a log like premade cookies. Refrigerate until firm before slicing.

Seafood Butter Sauce

2 sticks butter, melted
¼ cup white wine vinegar
1 teaspoon onion flakes
Salt and pepper to taste

In a saucepan over medium-low heat, melt butter. Stir in remaining ingredients until mixed well. Remove from heat to cool. Serve warm or chilled over your favorite seafood.

Orange Kissed Cocktail Sauce

This cocktail sauce adds a bit of Florida citrus flavor to a classic cocktail sauce.

1½ cups ketchup
¼ cup prepared horseradish
2 tablespoons orange juice, or to taste
½ tablespoon soy sauce or Worcestershire sauce
2 teaspoons freshly squeezed lemon or lime juice
2 teaspoons hot sauce

Combine all ingredients in a glass bowl; mix, chill and serve.

Ally's Homemade Cocktail Sauce

Ally's favorite way to eat oysters is topped with her Homemade Cocktail Sauce. During one visit to Mexico Beach, Florida, she convinced the owner of a small local restaurant that they should be making fresh cocktail sauce. They mixed up several versions right there at the table for a quick taste-testing.

1 cup ketchup
1 lemon, juiced
1½ tablespoons horseradish
3 teaspoons Worcestershire sauce
3 dashes hot sauce, or to taste

Combine all ingredients in a glass bowl; mix, chill and serve.

Seafood Cocktail Sauce

⅔ cup ketchup
2 tablespoons steak sauce
1 tablespoon prepared horseradish
½ fresh lemon, juiced
½ tablespoon hot sauce
Salt and pepper to taste

Thoroughly mix all ingredients; cover. Chill; serve cold with boiled or fried seafood.

Two Easy Tartar Sauces

Here is a very simple recipe for a tartar sauce that's more traditional in flavor as well as one that has a bit more kick to it.

Basic Tartar Sauce:

⅔ cup mayonnaise
¼ cup sour cream
1 tablespoon sweet relish
2 to 3 teaspoons seafood seasoning

In a glass bowl, combine all ingredients; cover and chill.

Spicy Version:

Basic Tartar Sauce
¼ cup hot sauce
¼ cup chopped onion
1 tablespoon Cajun seasoning
½ tablespoon minced jalapeño pepper
Dash lemon or lime juice

Start with the Basic Tartar Sauce recipe. Stir in remaining ingredients. Refrigerate 1 hour or longer. Serve chilled with your favorite seafood.

Coastal Tartar Sauce with Capers

I suggest making this recipe the day you plan on using it because the citrus juice and other ingredients will start breaking down the mayonnaise.

4 small dill pickles, finely chopped
¼ cup finely chopped fresh parsley leaves
1 tablespoon finely chopped capers
1 clove minced garlic
2 teaspoons orange juice
1 teaspoon lemon juice
1 teaspoon salt
1 teaspoon cracked black pepper
1 cup mayonnaise
1 tablespoon sour cream

Combine pickles, parsley, capers and garlic in a bowl along with orange juice, lemon juice, salt and black pepper. Stir in mayonnaise and sour cream; mix well. Chill before serving. Use same day and discard left overs.

Lemon-Lime Tequila Sauce

This Lemon-Lime Tequila Sauce has a bit more zest than a normal dipping sauce. It's perfect with seafood and chicken.

1 cup clear tequila
2 tablespoons lime juice
2 tablespoons lemon juice
2 green onions, finely chopped
½ tablespoon minced garlic
2 teaspoons cilantro
Salt and ground black pepper to taste
¾ cup heavy cream
1 stick butter, sliced
Dash hot sauce

Place all ingredients in a saucepan over medium-high heat. Bring to a boil and continue to boil 5 minutes. Reduce heat to medium and continue to cook until mixture reduces by a third. Cool and use immediately or chill, covered, until ready to use. Reheat before serving with your favorite seafood or chicken.

Quick Honey Mustard Tartar Dipping Sauce

1 cup mayonnaise
3 tablespoons Dijon mustard
1½ tablespoons sweet pickle relish
1 tablespoon minced onion
2 to 3 teaspoons honey
Dash black pepper

In a lidded bowl, thoroughly mix all ingredients; cover. Chill at least 30 minutes before serving.

Florida Maritime Museum

Located in the historic fishing village of Cortez, Florida, Florida Maritime Museum is housed in a 1912 schoolhouse featuring a number of permanent collections as well as temporary exhibits. The history of the area and the Cortez Fishing Village is prominently displayed as well as the history of Florida's Gulf Coast. The permanent collections include an exhibit of seashells that show the natural colors and shapes that are often missing from shells baked in the sun and found on a beach. The facility also houses a growing collection of model boats, historical artifacts, photographs, and more that help tell the story of the area and life in a real fishing village that has survived hurricanes and the Great Depression. This unique museum features a rather large outreach program that includes special events ranging from "Music on the Porch," to guest speakers, history classes, maritime skill classes, living history demonstrations, and even "Yoga at the Museum."

Florida Maritime Museum

4415 119th Street West • Cortez, Florida 34215
(941) 708-6120 • www.floridamaritimemuseum.org

Homemade Florida Orange Powder

The great news is that this oven-dehydrating method works with oranges, tangerines, cuties, lemons, limes and even pineapples. Dried citrus powder can be added to just about any seafood recipe with great results. Citrus powders are also perfect for riming beverage glasses for beach-inspired drinks.

4 oranges
Wax paper
Cookie sheet
2 teaspoons sugar
½ teaspoon salt

Preheat oven to 200°. Carefully slice oranges as thinly as possible (there's no need to peel them) using a knife, slicer or mandolin. Slices should be no thicker than ¼ of an inch. Discard top and bottom pieces. Lay slices on wax paper-covered cookie sheets or on cookie sheets using a wire rack. (Do not overlap the slices.) Place pans in center of oven; bake 3 hours. The goal is to dry out the moisture without turning the slices brown or burning any edges which can cause a burned or bitter taste. Remove dried oranges from oven and set aside to cool completely. Place dried slices in a spice grinder or food processor with sugar and salt; grind into a fine powder.

Bayou Seafood Seasoning

3 tablespoons paprika
2 tablespoons garlic powder
1½ tablespoons salt
1½ tablespoons onion powder
1 tablespoon dried oregano
1 tablespoon dried thyme
1 tablespoon cayenne pepper
½ tablespoon chili powder
½ tablespoon pepper

Combine all ingredients in a bowl. Process in a spice grinder or food processor to a consistent powder. Store in a dry container in a cool, dry place until ready to use; stores well.

Homemade Gulf Coast Citrus Seafood Seasoning

1½ tablespoons celery salt
1 tablespoon ground bay leaves
1 tablespoon orange powder (page 156)
3 teaspoons black pepper
3 teaspoons paprika
1 teaspoon dry mustard
½ teaspoon chili powder
¼ teaspoon ground nutmeg
¼ teaspoon cinnamon powder
¼ teaspoon ground cloves

Grind all ingredients in a spice grinder or food processor. Store in an airtight container in a cool, dry place until ready to use.

Coastal Tex-Mex Seasoning Mix

2½ tablespoons chili powder
2½ tablespoons paprika
2 tablespoons ground cumin
1¼ tablespoons salt
1 tablespoon garlic powder
1 tablespoon onion powder
1 tablespoon ground coriander
3 teaspoons seafood seasoning
2 teaspoons cayenne pepper

Combine all ingredients in a bowl; mix well. Store in an airtight container in a cool, dry place.

Apple Strawberry Smoothie

1½ cups frozen strawberries
1 (6-ounce) carton berry-flavored yogurt
1 banana, peeled
1 cup apple juice
3 cups ice

Combine in a blender; mix until smooth. Serve cold.

Gulf Coast Orange Smoothie

2 oranges peeled
1 (6-ounce) carton yogurt
1 cup skim milk
4 cups ice

Combine in a blender; mix until smooth. Serve cold.

Toasted Coconut Pineapple Smoothie

A quick and easy smoothie recipe that uses up some of the coconut flakes you've had in the freezer since you made cookies. This recipe makes two generous servings. A dash of flavored rum is optional.

½ to ¾ cup coconut flakes
2 cups milk
2 cups plain or citrus-flavored yogurt
1 (8-ounce) can crushed pineapple, with juice
½ teaspoon vanilla
10 to 12 ice cubes

Toast coconut flakes in oven or toaster oven until edges are slightly golden. Combine all ingredients in a blender. Blend until smooth; serve cold.

Pineapple Smoothie

1 (8-ounce) can pineapple chunks
1½ cups skim milk
1 cup vanilla yogurt
1 banana, peeled
¼ cup shaved coconut
1 tablespoon honey
Dash orange juice
3 cups ice

Combine in a blender; mix until smooth. Serve cold.

Banana Topping

2 semi-ripe bananas
1½ teaspoons cinnamon powder
1 tablespoon brown sugar
1 (16-ounce) can vanilla icing
1 (8-ounce) carton whipped topping

Mash bananas into a paste; stir in cinnamon and brown sugar. Open icing; fluff with a fork. In a bowl, fold together icing, whipped topping and bananas. Spread over chocolate muffins, cupcakes, cake or whatever suits you.

Grilled Bananas

5 bananas
½ cup cream of coconut
1½ tablespoons pineapple juice
1 tablespoon brown sugar
½ cup shredded coconut
Spiced rum (optional)

Peel bananas and cut lengthwise. Mix remaining ingredients. Place bananas on nonstick foil treaded with nonstick spray. Grill over medium-high heat, about 4 to 5 minutes on each side. Top with coconut mixture; continue to grill until coconut turns slightly brown. You can also add a bit of spiced rum, if you desire.

Coastal Sunshine Orange Squares

1 (14-ounce) can sweetened condensed milk
½ cup orange juice
1½ cups graham cracker crumbs
¾ cup all-purpose flour
⅓ cup brown sugar
½ teaspoon baking powder
Dash salt
½ cup butter, melted

Combine milk and orange juice. Mix well; set aside. In a separate bowl, combine crumbs, flour, sugar, baking powder and salt. Stir in butter until crumbly. Press half into a greased 9-inch square pan. Spread lemon mixture over crumbs. Top with remaining crumbs. Bake at 375° for 20 to 25 minutes. Cool before slicing.

Acadian Village

When visiting Acadian Village you may have the feeling you've stepped back in time. In the 1970's, officials with the Lafayette Association for Retarded Citizens started planning possible uses for a portion of their 32 acres of property. Their goals were to increase tourism, generate needed capital for the LARC, and employ those with developmental disabilities that were fully capable of working. Period buildings were purchased, or donated, and carefully moved piece by piece to the ten acre site, then carefully restored. Additional buildings were constructed on site, and the beautiful bayou-style waterway running through the village is man-made. The work was done by local craftsmen, business leaders and volunteers, as well as U.S. Army Reservists. The result is an 1800's Cajun village complete with gift shop, tours, living history events, and more. Acadian Village now serves as an amazing history learning site as well as a favorite location for Cajun festivals, weddings, special events, corporate functions, and an annual Christmas event.

Acadian Village

200 Greenleaf Drive • Lafayette, Louisiana 70506
(337) 981-2364 • www.acadianvillage.org

Coastal Key Lime Pie with Chocolate

5 tablespoons butter, melted
1½ cups graham cracker crumbs
½ cup finely chopped almonds
1 (14-ounce) can sweetened condensed milk
½ cup Key lime or lime juice
2 teaspoons grated lime zest, divided
2 eggs, separated
¼ teaspoon cream of tartar
¼ cup sugar
Chocolate hard shell for topping

In a bowl, mix butter, crumbs and almonds by hand. Pat crust mix into a pie pan. Bake 5 to 10 minutes at 350°. In a medium bowl, combine milk, lime juice and 1 teaspoon zest; blend in egg yolks. Pour filling into crust. Beat egg whites with cream of tartar until soft peaks form. Gradually beat in sugar and remaining teaspoon zest until mixture is stiff. Spread meringue over filling; spread to seal edges. Bake 12 to 15 minutes, or until meringue is golden brown. Allow pie to cool in refrigerator; top with hard shell chocolate topping.

Key Lime Cake

All of my friends know I am a sucker for Key lime pie. So when I tried some Key lime cake at a restaurant along the coast, I was bound and determined to make one. Here it is.

4 eggs
1 cup water
1 cup vegetable oil
⅓ cup plus 3 tablespoons Key lime juice, divided
1 (3.4-ounce) box lemon instant pudding
1 (18.25-ounce) box lemon cake mix
2 cups powdered sugar
¼ cup chopped coconut (optional)

In a bowl, beat eggs; add water, oil, 3 tablespoons lime juice, instant pudding and cake mix, beating with electric mixer until well blended. Cook in greased and floured cake pans or in a glass cake dish. Cook for 1 hour at 325°. Combine powdered sugar, coconut and remaining lime juice; mix well. Spread over cooled cake.

Recipe Listing

Seafood

Alligator:

Grilled Gator Bites with Tangy Orange Dipping Sauce 28

Southern Fried Alligator 30

Clams:

Baked Gulf Clams with White Wine Butter Sauce and Rustic Potatoes 110

Conch:

Ally's Key West Inspired Conch Fritter 18

Continued on next page...

Crab:

Blue Crab Salad Sandwich 50

Coastal Crab Dip 14

Coastal Crab Gumbo 33

Crab Coleslaw Salad 134

Crab Jalapeño Poppers 12

Crabmeat Balls 24

Easy Coastal Seafood Chowder 34

Fried Blue Crabs 127

Fried Gulf Coast Crabs 128

Mississippi Mashed Seafood Tater Tots 25

Seafood Paté 15

Seafood Po-Boy 44

Slightly Spicy Panko Crab Cakes 26

Spicy Crab Soup 35

Stone Crab Claws with Pineapple Sauce 130

Tapas-Style Creole Crab Balls with Dijon Rémoulade Sauce 22

Texas Coast Tortilla Chip Crab Cakes 27

Crawfish:

Bayou Big Easy Crawfish Alfredo 56

Crawdaddy's Gumbo 32

Easy Crawfish and Black Bean Nachos 17

Fish:

Baked Chili Lime Wahoo Tostados 76

Baked Pompanos with Pineapple and Mango Salsa 91

Beach Grouper Packs 64

Biloxi Bacon Po-Boy with Fried Pickles and Jalapeños 40

Biloxi Beer-Battered Hot Fish Fillets 68

Blackened Catfish Hoagie with Creole Mustard Sauce 42

Blackened Fish 69

Cedar Plank Grilled Cobia 70

Coastal Fried Catfish 97

Creole Baked Redfish with Tangy Chili Mayo 73

Crunchy Grilled Snapper Burritos with Avacado Mayo 74

Easy Coastal Seafood Chowder 34

Fish Tacos 81

Grilled Amberjack Fillets with Toasted Corn and Black Bean Salsa 84

Grilled Zesty Shark Steaks with Easy Pineapple Salsa 136

Gulf Coast Classic Fish and Seasoned Chips 98

Jerk Rubbed Black Drum with Easy Black Beans and Rice 82

Lemon Pepper Amberjack 83

Marinated Swordfish Salad 39

Open-Faced Halibut Sandwiches with Peach and Mango Salsa 48

Oven Fried Grouper Fillets with Seasoned Baked Chips 100

Pineapple Rum Grouper Cheddar Melts with Spicy Apricot Dipping Sauce 46

Red Snapper Pimento Cheese with Bacon and Jalapeños 16

Seafood Po-Boy 44

Seafood Paté 15

Seared Coconut Rum Grouper 88

Seaside Fish Tenders 102

Southern Fried Hot Fish with Cornbread Salad 104

Spotted Sea Trout with Sriracha Lime Mayonnaise 66

Sweet Buttermilk Mullet Fritters 20

Thai Swordfish Steaks with Five Spice Quinoa 94

Wasabi Seared Tuna 92

Whiskey Glazed Cast-Iron Amberjack Fillets 87

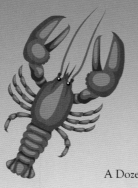

Lobster:

Florida Lobster Tails 135

Oysters:

A Dozen Raw Oysters on the Half Shell 106

Fried Apalachicola Oysters 107

Gulf Coast Oysters Rockefeller 108

Scallops:

Broiled Scallop and Portabella Mushroom Salad 38

Italian Bay Scallops and Shrimp with Wild Rice 132

Key West Scallop and Chicken Tomato Pasta 58

Mexico Beach Butter Scallops 60

Shrimp:

Cape San Blas Shrimp Wings 10

Creole Shrimp and Biscuits 122

Easy Bayou-Style Boiled Shrimp 116

Easy Coastal Seafood Chowder 34

Easy Gulf Coast Shrimp Sliders 51

Foil Pack Shrimp Boil 117

Grilled Italian Bay Scallops and Shrimp with Wild Rice 132

Gulf Coast Chopped Shrimp Bisque 36

Gulf Coast Shrimp Jambalaya 63

Italian Bay Scallops and Shrimp with Wild Rice 132

Kent's Shrimp, Chicken and Sausage Jambalaya 62

Macee's Battered Popcorn Shrimp 125

Minced Gulf Shrimp Burgers 52

Palm Harbor Garlic Shrimp 118

Seafood Po-Boy 44

Shrimp and Cheese Grits 121

Shrimp and Veggie Pizza 115

Shrimp Naan Bread Pizza with Ricotta Sauce 112

Spicy Shrimp Tacos with Easy Texas Tartar Sauce 78

Texas Coast Shrimp Scampi 55

Time Saver Pesto Shrimp and Pasta 56

Whole Gulf Shrimp Spring Rolls 11

Little Something Extra

Flavored Butter:

Sauces and Seasonings:

Side Dishes:

Smoothies:

Desserts:

Travel Destinations

Alabama:

Gulf Shores, Fort Morgan

Mobile, GulfQuest: National Maritime Museum of the Gulf of Mexico

Mobile, USS Alabama Battleship Memorial Park

Florida:

Cortez, Florida Maritime Museum

Key West, Dry Tortugas National Park

Pensacola, Historic Pensacola

Louisiana:

Lafayette, Acadian Village

New Orleans, Fort Pike

Mississippi:

Biloxi, Biloxi Lighthouse

Gulfport, Fort Massachusetts

Texas:

Galveston, Bishop's Palace

Houston, The 1940 Air Terminal Museum

Museum Ships of the Gulf Coast States

Alabama

USS Alabama BB-60, Dakota Class WWII Battleship
Battleship Memorial Park, Mobile

USS Drum SS-228, Balo Class WWII Submarine
Battleship Memorial Park, Mobile

Florida

SS American Victory, WWII Victory Ship
American Victory Ship Mariners Memorial Museum, Tampa

USCGC Ingham WHEC-35, WWII Coast Guard Cutter
USCGC Ingham Memorial Museum, Key West

Louisiana

USS Kidd DD-661, WWII Fletcher-class destroyer
USS Kidd Veterans Museum, Baton Rouge

USS Orleck DD-886, WWII Gearing-class destroyer
USS Orleck Naval Museum, Lake Charles

Mississippi

USS Cairo, Civil War Ironclad
USS Cairo Gunboat and Museum, Vicksburg (inland)

Texas

USS Cavalla SS-244, Gato Class WWII Submarine
Seawolf Park, Galveston

Elissa, Three-Masted Barque Sailing Ship
Texas Seaport Museum, Galveston

HA. 19, Japanese Midget Submarine
National Museum of the Pacific War, Fredericksburg (inland)

USS Lexington CV-16, WWII Essex Class Aircraft Carrier
USS LEXINGTON Museum on the Bay, Corpus Christi

USS Stewart DE-238, WWII Edsall Class Destroyer Escort
Seawolf Park, Galveston

USS Texas BB-35, New York Class Battleship
San Jacinto Battleground State Historic Site, La Porte

Little Gulf Coast makes a Great Gift

EACH: $14.95 • 192 pages • 5½x8½
paperbound • full-color

Eat & Explore State Cookbook Series

EACH: $18.95 • 256 pages • 7x9
paperbound • full-color

**Arkansas • Illinois • Minnesota
North Carolina • Ohio
Oklahoma •Virginia • Washington**

Experience our United States like never before when you explore the distinct flavor of each state by savoring 250 favorite recipes from the state's best cooks. In addition, the state's favorite events and destinations are profiled throughout the book with fun stories and everything you need to know to plan your family's next road trip.

Great American Grilling

EACH: $21.95 • 288 pages • 7x10
paperbound • full-color

Also by Kent Whitaker

The Ultimate Venison Cookbook for Deer Camp

EACH: $21.95 • 288 pages • 7x10
paperbound • full-color

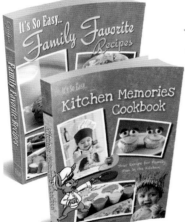

It's So Easy to Cook Food Your Family Will Love

EACH: $18.95 • 256 pages • 7x10
paperbound • full-color

Church Recipes are the Best

Georgia Church Suppers
$18.95 • 256 pages • 7x10 • paperbound • full-color

Mississippi Church Suppers
$21.95 • 288 pages • 7x10 • paperbound • full-color

State Hometown Cookbook Series

EACH: $18.95 • 256 pages • 7x10 or 8x9
paperbound • full-color

3 Easy Ways to Order

1) Call toll-free **1-888-854-5954** to order by phone or to request a free catalog.

2) Order online at **www.GreatAmericanPublishers.com**

3) Mail a check or money order for the cost of the book(s) plus $4 shipping for the first book and $1 each additional (6 or more = free shipping) plus a list of the books you want to order along with your name, address, phone and email to:

Great American Publishers
501 Avalon Way Suite B
Brandon MS 39047

Find us on facebook: www.facebook.com/GreatAmericanPublishers

Join the We Love 2 Cook Club and get a 20% discount.
www.GreatAmericanPublishers.com

A Hometown Taste of America, One State at a Time

**Alabama • Georgia • Louisiana Mississippi
South Carolina • Tennessee • Texas • West Virginia**

Florida Hometown Cookbook **coming soon...**

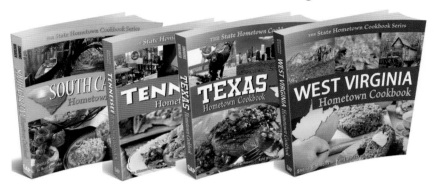

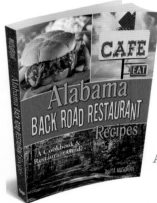

State Back Road
Restaurants Cookbook Series

EACH: $18.95 • 256 pages • 7x9
paperbound • full-color

Alabama • Kentucky • Missouri • Tennessee • Texas

May the God of hope fill you with all joy and peace as you trust in him, so that you may overflow with hope by the power of the Holy Spirit.

—Romans 15:13 (NIV)